AF255598

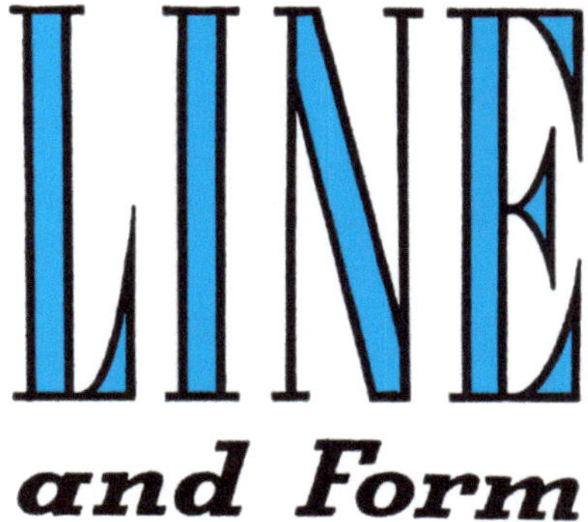
LINE
and Form

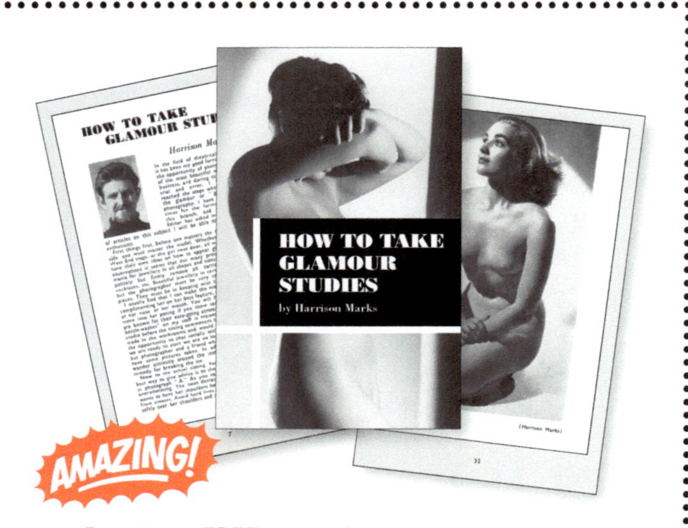

Receive a **FREE** copy of
How to take Glamour Studies by Harrison Marks
when you sign up to our mailing list at
www.pamela-green.com/mailing-list

Published in 2023 by Wolfbait Books

www.wolfbait.co.uk

ISBN: 9781999744137

Below: Rosa Domaille.

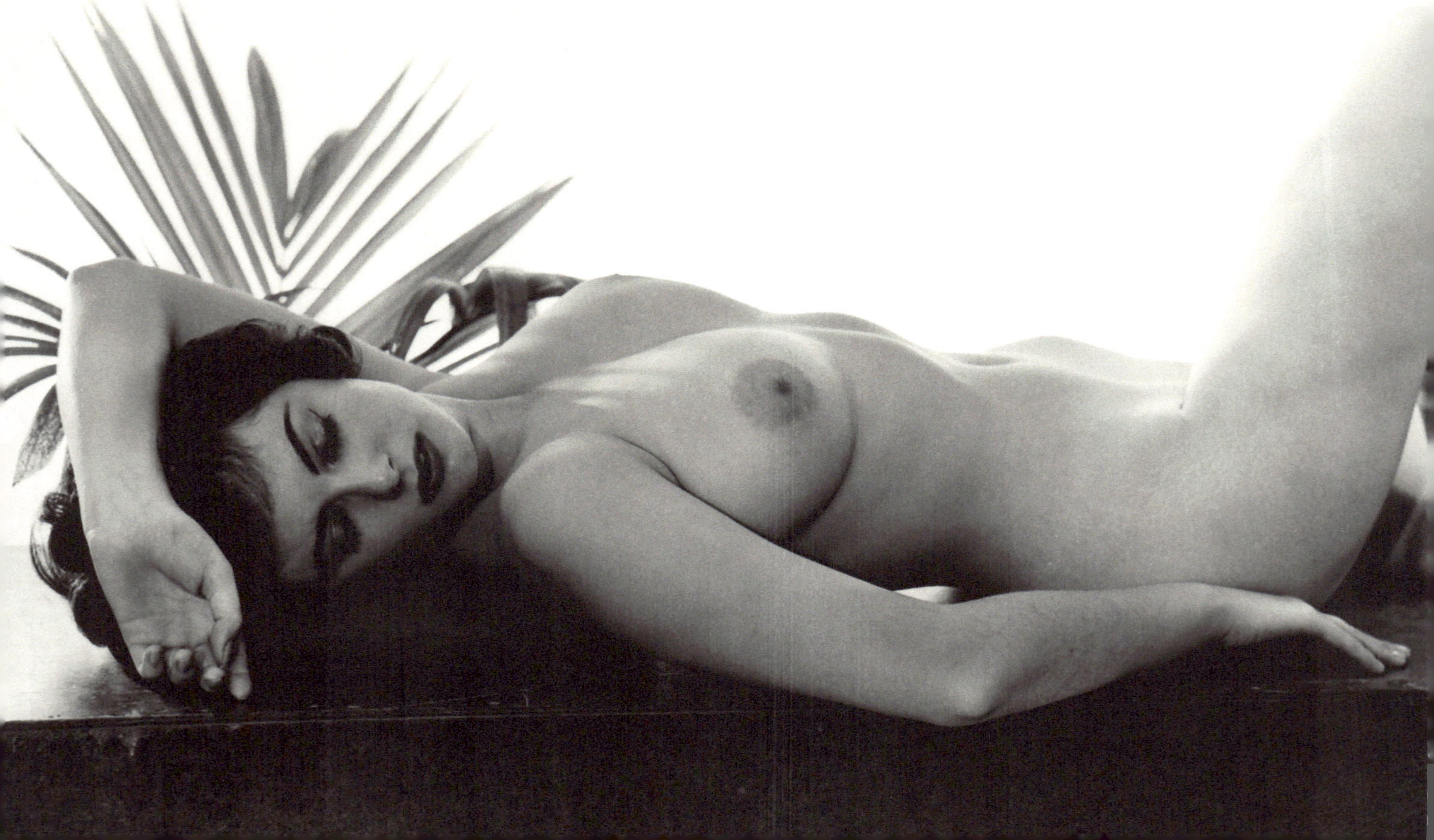

LINE
and Form

By Yahya El-Droubie

Photography by Eva Grant

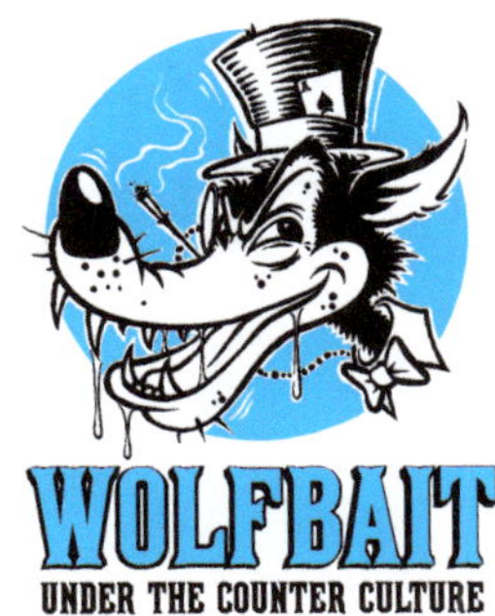

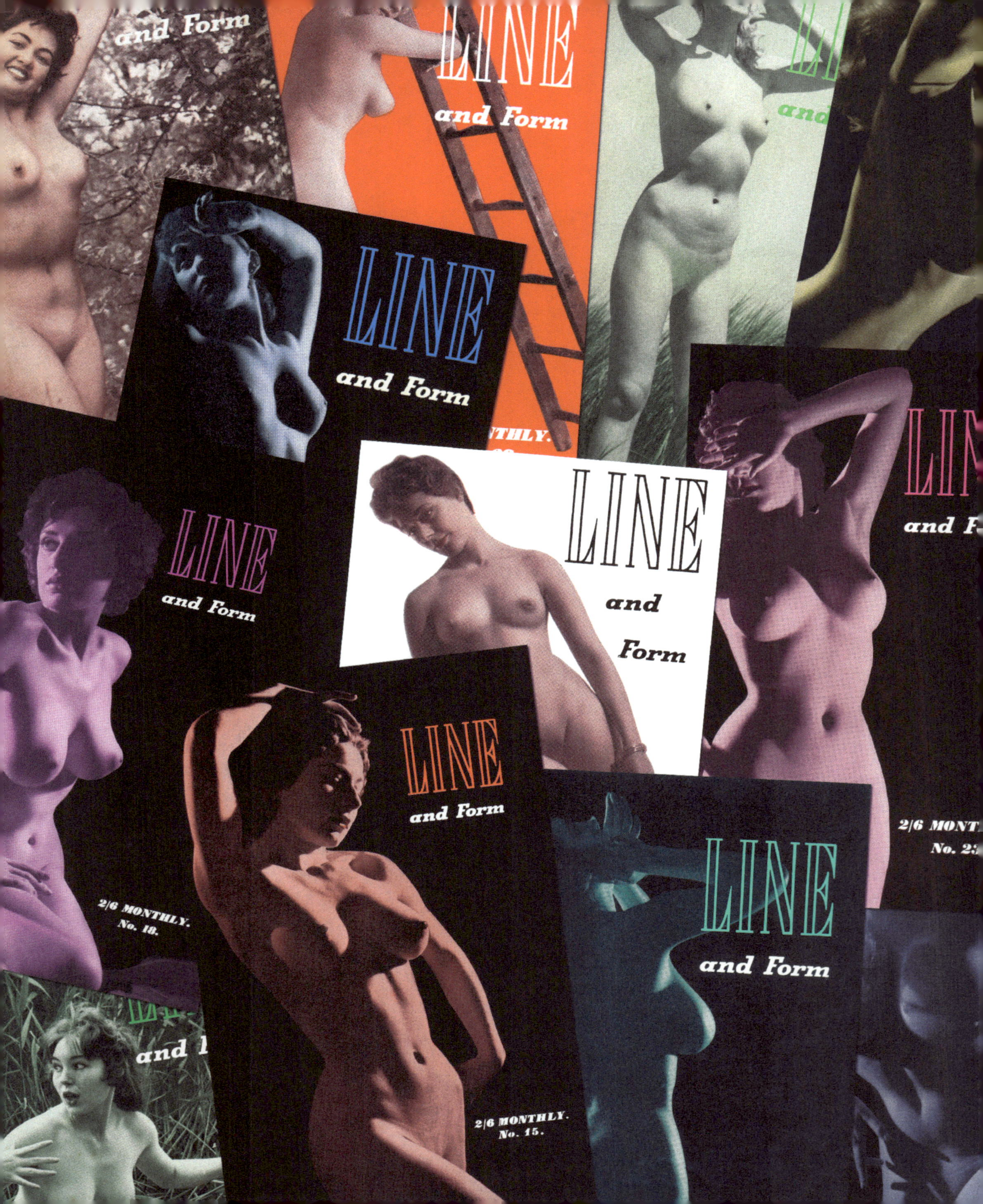

Publishing Nude Studies

FOR FOUR DECADES from the end of the First World War to the beginning of the 1960s, over-the-counter magazines that specialised in nudity were dominated by two types: those aimed at art students without access to life models, and body culture magazines often intended to promote the nudist movement.

It's long been assumed that these publications were produced by "smut peddlers" or opportunists trying to circumvent censorship; however, this is an inaccurate oversimplification. Utopians, free thinkers, reformists and artists all played a role in the cultural response to the horrors of the First World War, the rise of mass consumerism and the impact of the industrialization and urbanization of society. The US magazine *Playboy*, which was launched in 1953, even made a positive contribution to the Civil Rights movement and the sexual revolution, aspects of its influence that are deliberately sidelined or denied to fit modern narratives.

The early issues of the US magazine *Figure* captured a moment in history when figure photography unashamedly strove to sit at the top table of art. Within its pages, nudes by photographers Zoltan Glass and Eva Grant sit comfortably alongside articles about artists such as Eric Gill and Henry Moore. The Greek photographer Eva Grant, a rare female working in the glamour field, launched her own magazine in Britain in the late 1950s, called *Line and Form*. While *Figure* magazine had declared that "From the earliest artistic expression of man through the greatest age of the arts, the Renaissance, and unto today, the beautiful lines of a beautiful woman have remained the alpha and omega of what is art," Grant herself stated that "From the time of the Greek sculptors until today, the presentation of grace in the plastic arts has depended much on the line and form of the female figure. There is a good reason for it. Whereas other art forms are limited in their initial concept, the intrinsic beauty of this alone has an infinite variety that age cannot weary nor custom stale." (See Wolfbait's *The Glamour Camera of Eva Grant* for a biography of Grant and more examples of her work.)

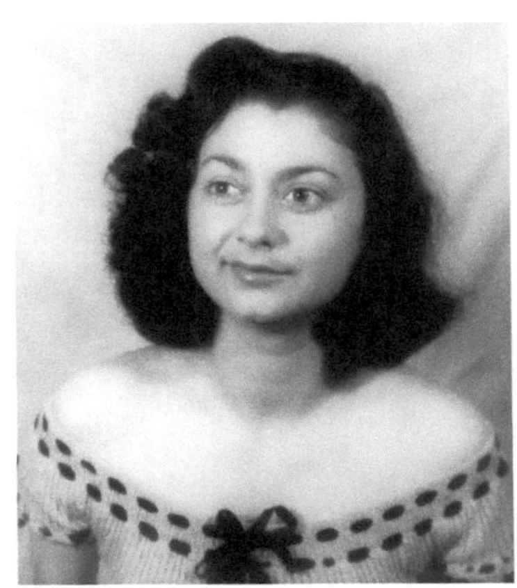

Above: Eva Grant.

Opposite: The early issues of *Line and Form* were printed and published by Gannet Press Ltd., 12 Market Place South, Birkenhead, after which the magazine was published by Photoform Publications Ltd., 13 Spring Street, London, W2. It was distributed by Rembooks Ltd., 102 Parkway, London, NW1, and printed by New Avenue Press Ltd., Eros Works, Spur Road, Bedfont, Middlesex. Photoform eventually changed its address to 196 Lancaster Road, London, W11.

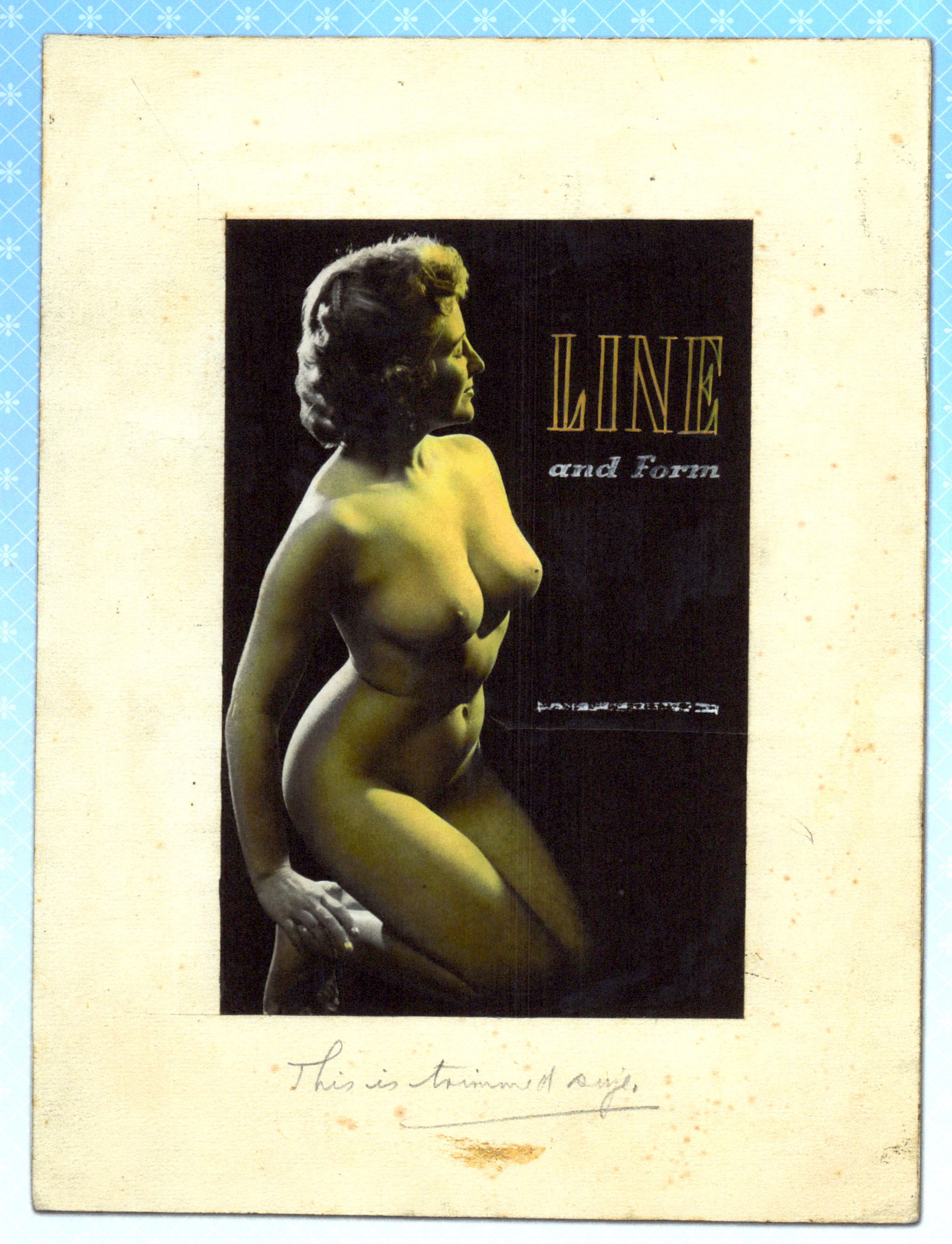

This is trimmed size.

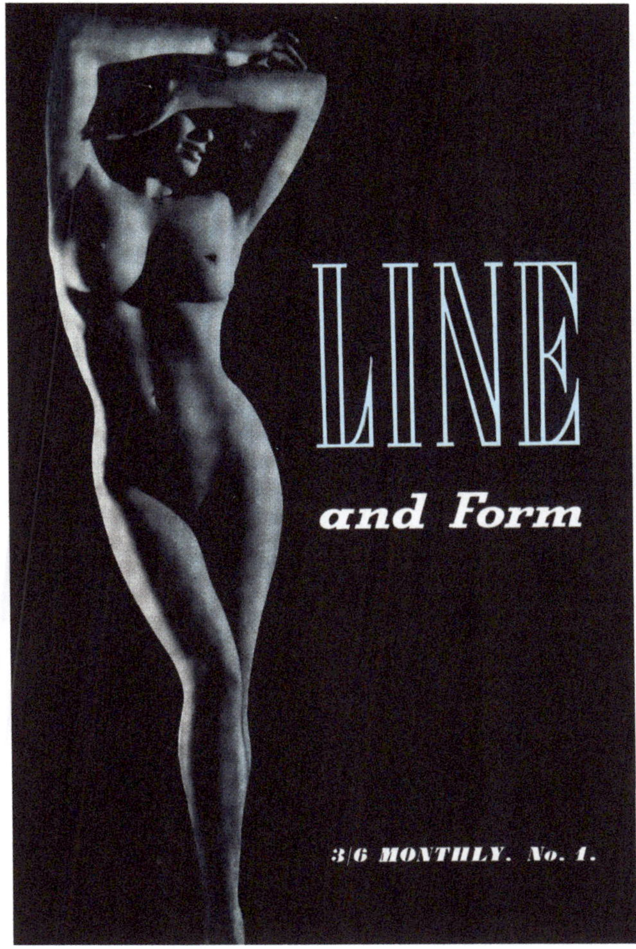

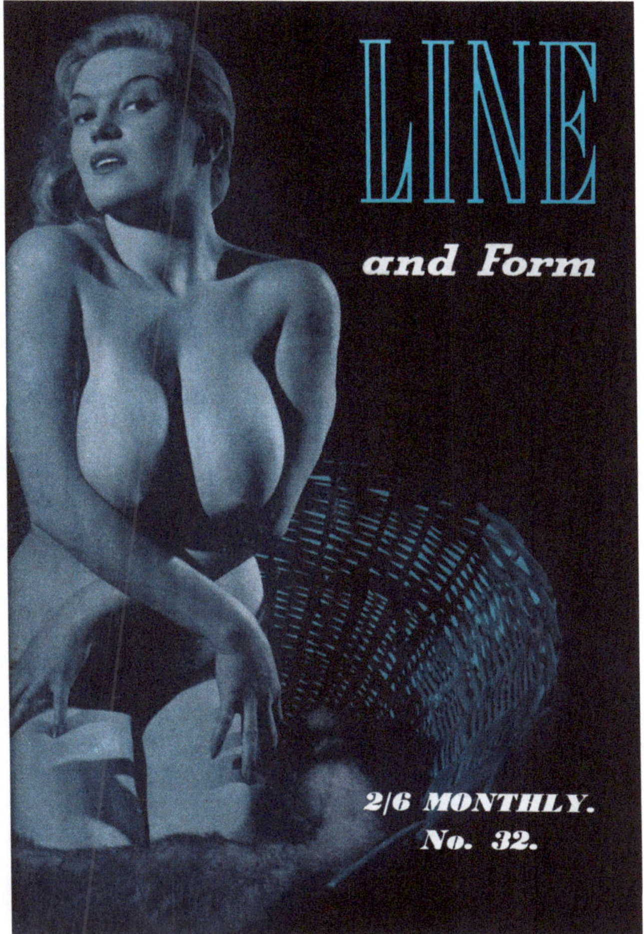

Line and Form was not the first magazine of its type in the UK. Arguably, that accolade goes to the partnership of Pamela Green and George Harrison Marks with their pocket magazine *Kamera*, launched in 1957. Like *Line and Form*, its format was 7 x 4.5 inches, with 30–40 pages in black and white and a colour cover. *Line and Form* ran for more than 40 issues and was produced under Eva Grant's own imprint, Photoform. The magazine's images were often accompanied by technical information, supposedly intended to assist photography students.

Many of the women Eva photographed for *Line and Form* were amateur models hoping to turn pro or typists wanting to earn a bit of extra money; several were dancers who Eva loved working with as they had a natural grace and could hold a pose. Several professional models posed for her, too, including Rosa Dolmai, June Palmer and Lee Sothern (aka Grace Jackson). The most collectable and rare issue of *Line and Form* is the 96-page *Leading Models from Line and Form*

Opposite: Hand-tinted cover artwork for *Line and Form* no. 5, featuring Norma Forrest.

Above left: *Line and Form* no. 1.

Above right: *Line and Form* no. 32, featuring the buxom Paula Page on the cover.

WATCH OUT
for
LINE *and* FORM No. 10
Ask your newsagent to keep a copy for you
_______NOW

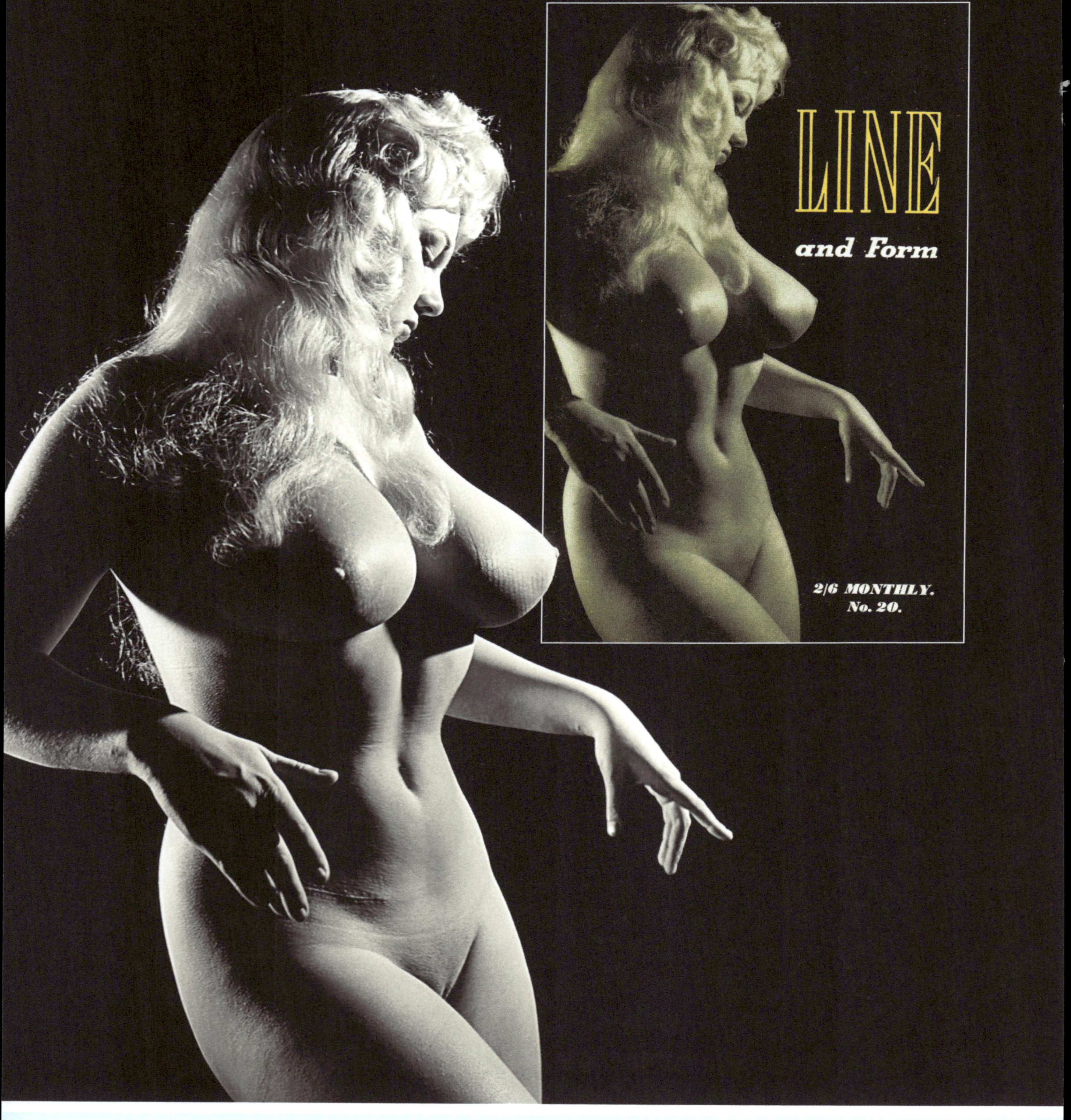
LINE
and Form
2/6 MONTHLY.
No. 20.

published by Gannet Press in 1957. Fourteen models, including fan favourites June Russell, Norma Forrest and Lee Sothern, were featured in its pages.

Alongside producing *Line and Form*, Eva Grant also worked for other companies, among them Axtell, who published *Foto*, and Arnold Book Co., who published *Photo Studio*. These magazines were more pin-up orientated, featuring swimsuit glamour and up-and-coming movie starlets, but they did have the occasional nude. "Through these pages pass the most beautiful girls in the world," ran the editorial for *Foto*, which was described as an international magazine of photographic art.

By the mid-1960s, the heyday of figure studies and innocent glamour work was over, and regrettably, Eva decided to call it a day. In time, her superb body of work was eclipsed in the history books by that of the male photographers – such as George Harrison Marks and Russell Gaye – who continued in the glamour field, an injustice that this book hopefully goes some way towards readdressing.

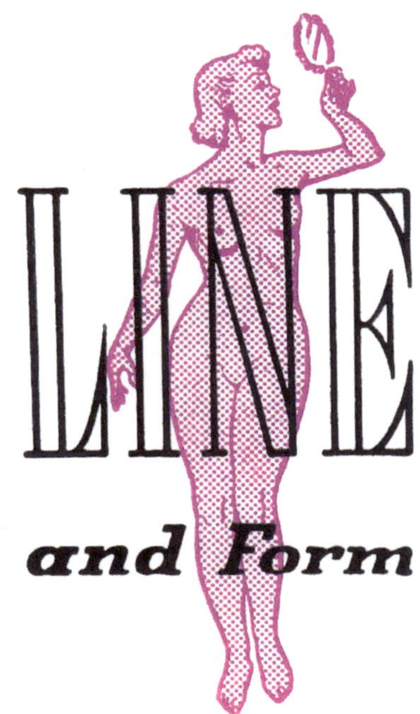

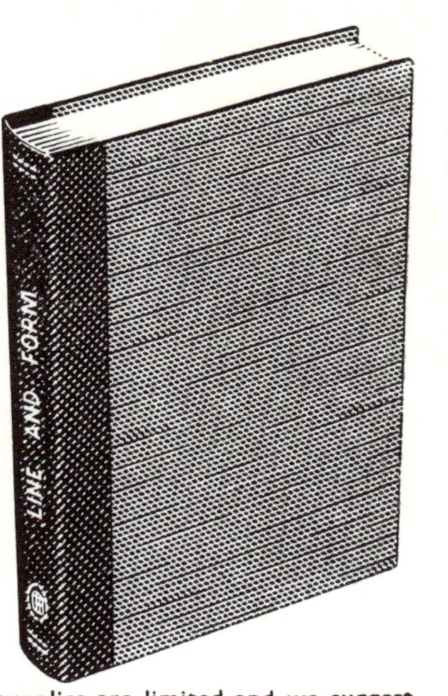

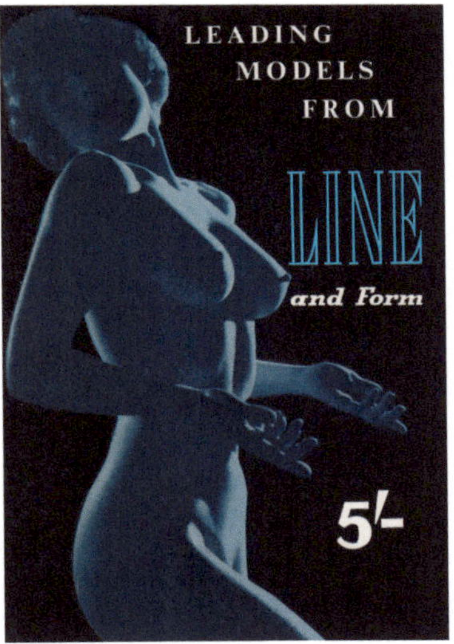

Top: *Line and Form* graphic motif.

Above: *Leading Models from Line and Form,* Gannet Press, 1957.

Left: Back cover advert for *Line and Form* holders.

Opposite: *Line and Form* no. 20, featuring Lorraine Burnett in a long blonde wig on the cover, along with the original photographic print.

Next Month's Line & Form

—make sure of it. How? Either hand this form to your newsagent as a notice to him that you want *Line & Form* regularly every month. Or have the magazine delivered direct by subscribing now. To:— 196 Lancaster Road, London, W.11.

Name: ....

ADDRESS: ....

12 ISSUES 30/-   8 ISSUES £1   4 ISSUES 10/-

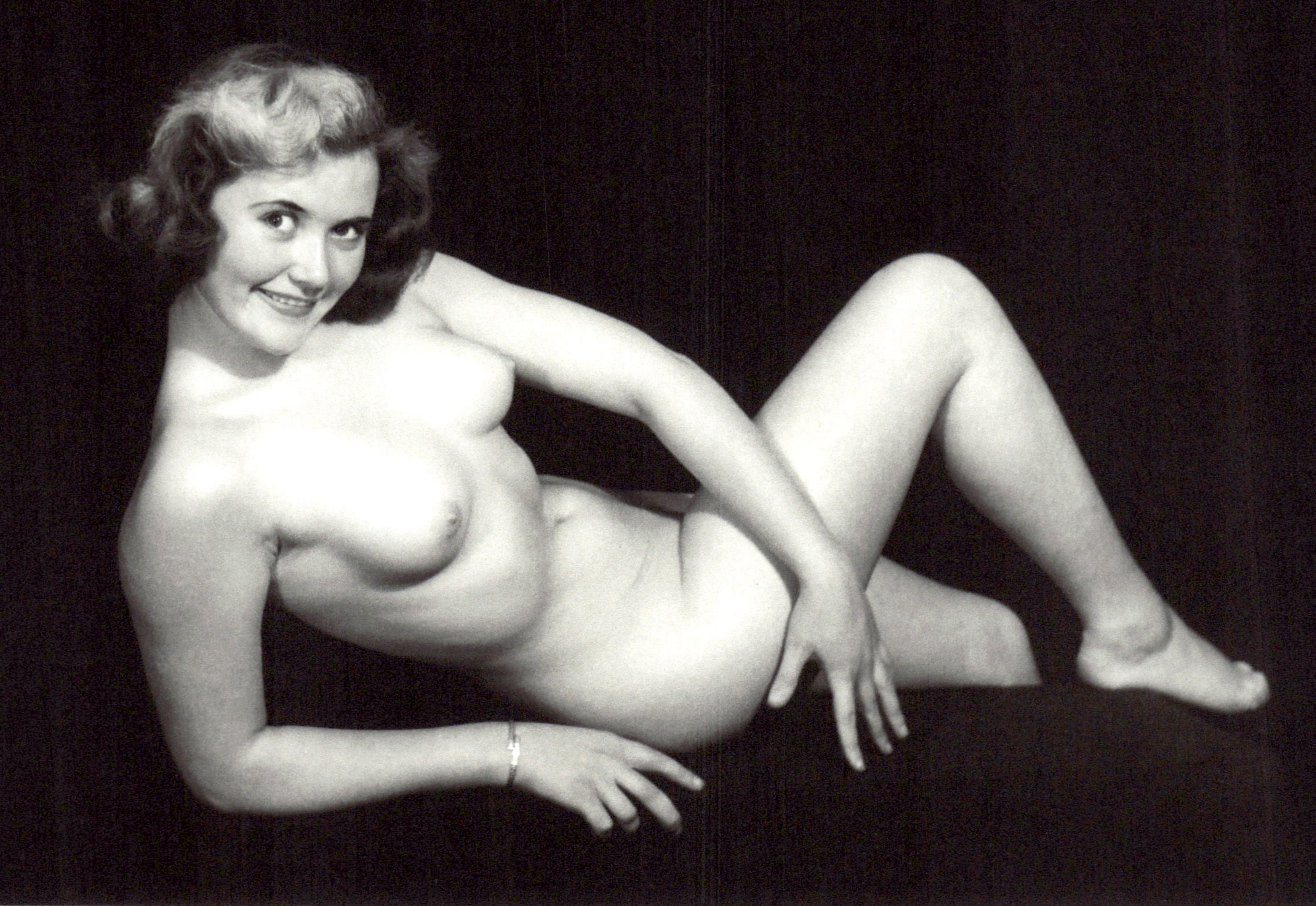

Above: Gloria Latham.

Opposite: The original typewritten manuscript for the editorial "Nudes and Props", in *Line and Form* no. 17, along with the cover (model, Janet Riley).

Editorial Nudes and Props
"Line and Form" No.17

Almost any single article can be used as a prop in figure photography, and generally, they fall into one of two classifications. They are either of the utility type, as typified by the box used in the study on page 6, or the chair in a study on page 10, or they are of the decorative type, such as the flower stand on page 21 or the twig and leaves on pages 26 and 27. However, no matter what purpose the props may serve, the important thing from the artist's point of view is that they should blend in with and supplement the figure to produce a picture which has more in it than merely a combination of model and props. If the picture the artist wishes to create is primarily a figure study, the props must only be used as a secondary and diminutive source of interest. They should, therefore, never have strong lines, and the lighting treatment of the prop itself should never be bolder than that of the model.

However, there is one very significant exception to this, which arises when the prop is used to suggest an abstract idea, such as the studies on pages 14 and 15 and those on pages 26 and 27. In all these pictures, the props are given the same treatment from a lighting point of view as the figures, but in each case, the contrast between the thin lines of the prop and the beautiful curves of the figures produces a picture with an atmosphere which is abstract and completely unrelated from either the figure or the props alone. In figure photography, a discreet prop can often be used to improve a picture's composition, providing that the prop is used discreetly and in context. Consider, for example, the study on page 25; this picture was initially taken as a pure study with no props, and the result was a model looking into an empty space. The picture was then re-taken, as shown on page 25, with the model looking at the book, and the result is the classic triangular composition which is much more pleasing than the original idea. The picture on page 12 portrays a similar type of composition. In the studies in this issue, items ranging from boxes to fishing nets have been successfully used as props, but in every case, the greatest possible care has been exercised to make sure that they become part of the picture, and in no single case have the props been used for their own sake.

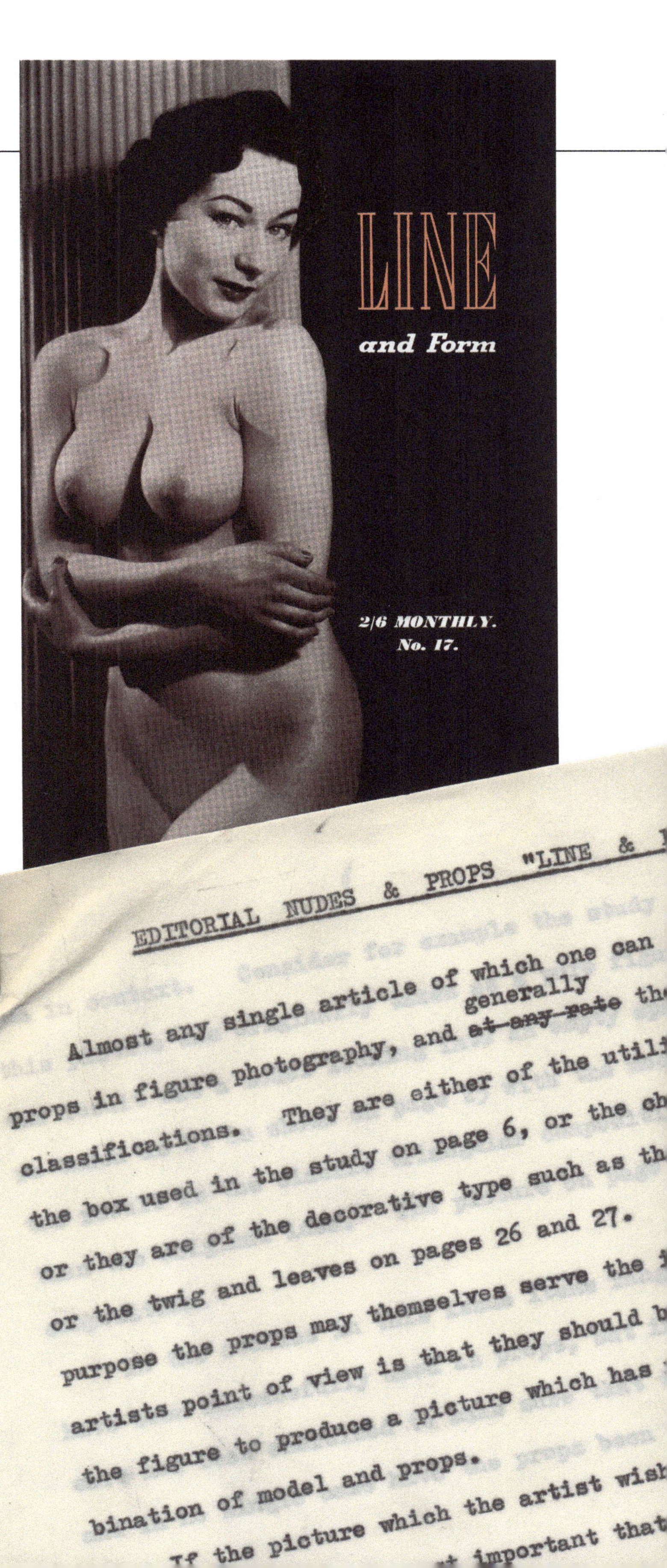

EDITORIAL NUDES & PROPS "LINE & F

Almost any single article of which one can generally props in figure photography, and ~~at any rate~~ the classifications. They are either of the utili the box used in the study on page 6, or the ch or they are of the decorative type such as th or the twig and leaves on pages 26 and 27. purpose the props may themselves serve the i artists point of view is that they should b the figure to produce a picture which has bination of model and props.

If the picture which the artist wish

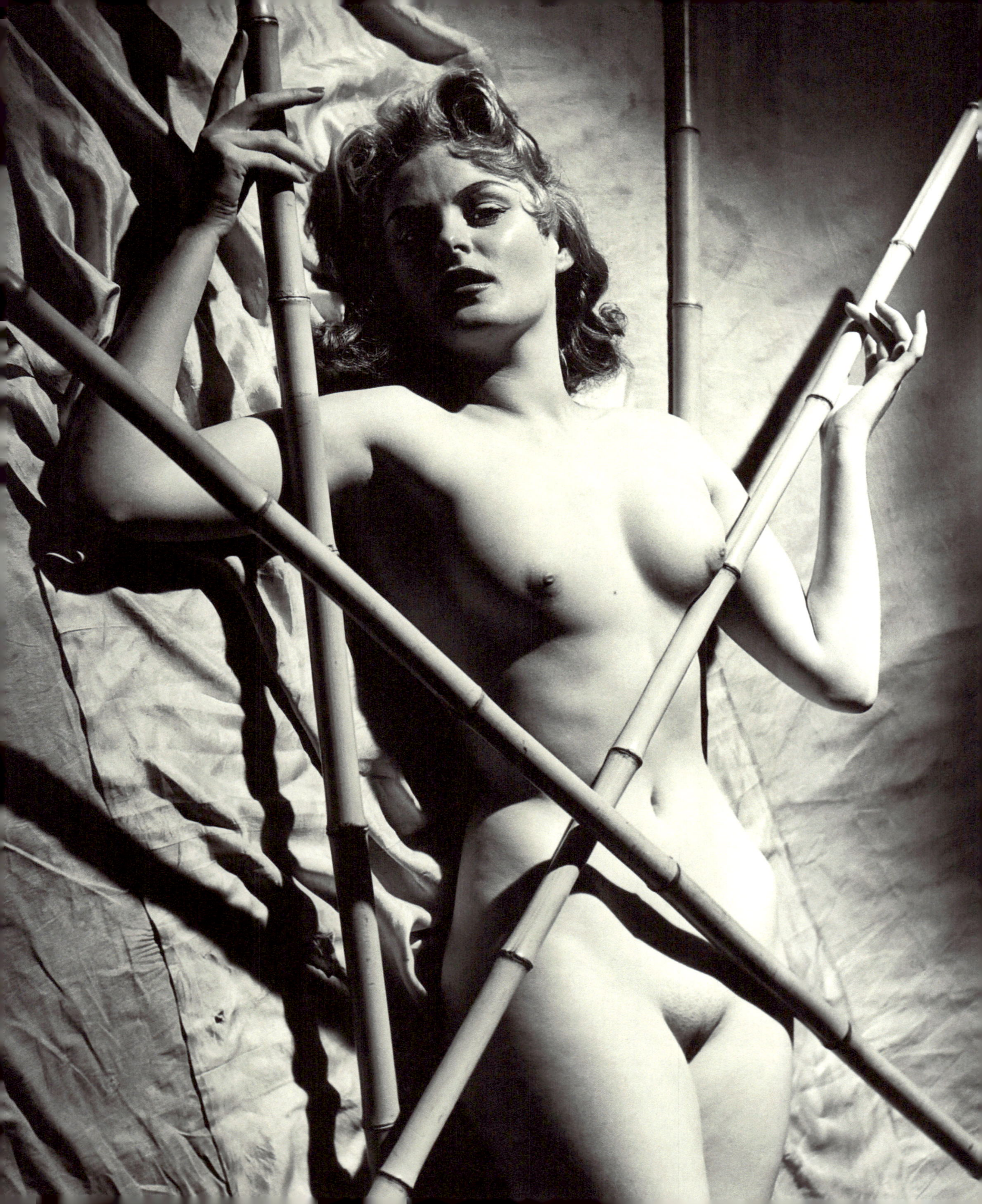

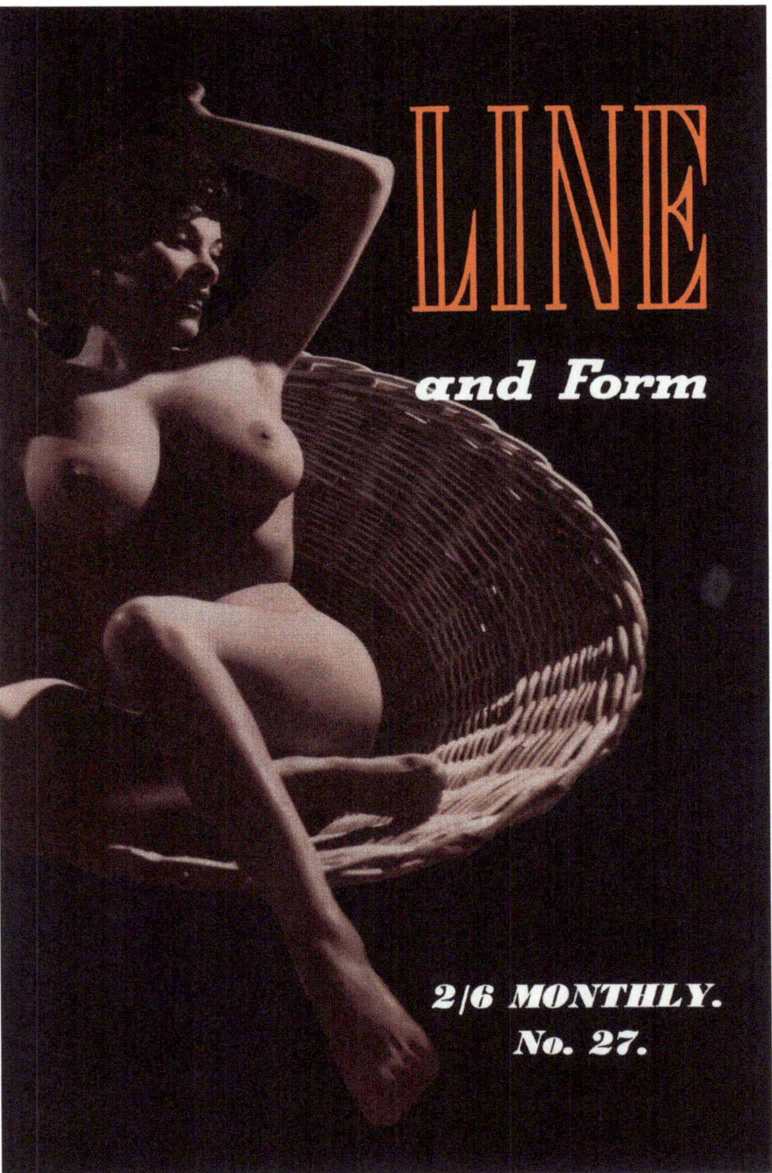

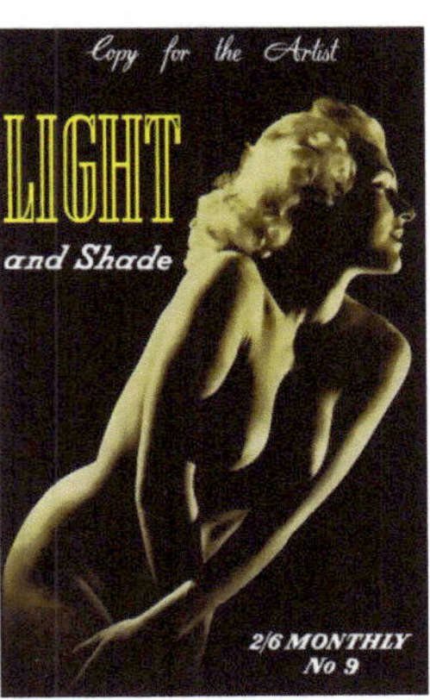

Opposite: Maxine Miller.

Above: *Line and Form* no. 27, featuring Sylvana Manto (Madelaine Bannister) on the cover.

Left: The magazine *Light and Shade*, produced by Russell Gay and published by Dalrow Publications Ltd., Pennine Publications, Bolton, used the same duotone effect on its cover as *Line and Form*. This, along with the similar title, led the magazines to be confused with one another.

Right: Two adverts that appeared in various issues of *Line and Form*.

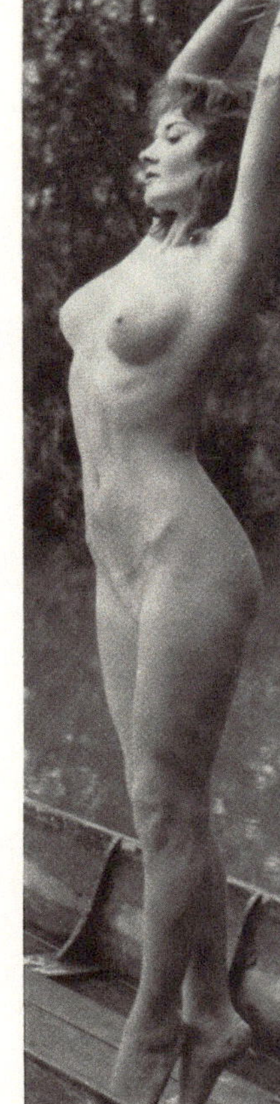

5′ 5½″
★★★★★★★★
TALL
★★★★★★★★★

Here's a fourth vital statistic: height. Vital? Well, wouldn't you like to own a thoroughly, exactly life-size photographic blowup of your favourite model?

You can—now. Beautifully produced by one of the leading photographic studios in Britain, a giant, life-size blowup of any girl in this issue of Line & Form is available for only five pounds, post free.

Your luxury print—all five feet plus of it—comes carefully sealed in a board cylinder within a few days of ordering. Simply send your cheque/money order/postal order/cash (cash in a registered envelope, please) with a note giving the page number of the print you want blown up to its true physical proportions.

Within a few days . . . she's yours.

Address orders to *Line & Form*, 196 Lancaster Road, London, W.11.

FREE- to our regular readers
ALBUM OF REAL PHOTOGRAPHS
OF THE COVER GIRL OF THIS ISSUE
LORRAINE BURNETT

This album consists of a number of real photographs of this glorious model, specially commissioned by *LINE AND FORM* and taken in Miss Burnett's own home. The photographs, each of which is a work of art, are bound together with plastic binding, into a beautiful album worth at least 10/-.

To get your album FREE all you have to do is to collect 3 coupons from this and the next two issues of *LINE AND FORM* and send them, with your name and address, to the publishers and you will receive by return of post your FREE ALBUM.

Place an order with your bookseller now to make sure that you get the next two issues of *LINE AND FORM*.

LINE AND FORM is published to fill the need of artists and photographers for a varied selection of photographic figure studies to supplement or take the place of the live model. These, with pertinent information on lighting, posing, proportion and so forth, make *LINE AND FORM* a 'must' to achieve and maintain proficiency in figure art.

PHOTOFORM PUBLICATIONS LTD., 13 Spring St., London, W.2

COUPON No. 1 for ALBUM OF REAL PHOTOGRAPHS OF LORRAINE BURNETT

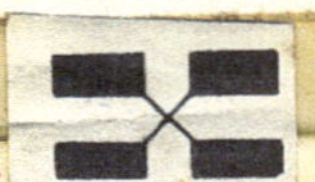
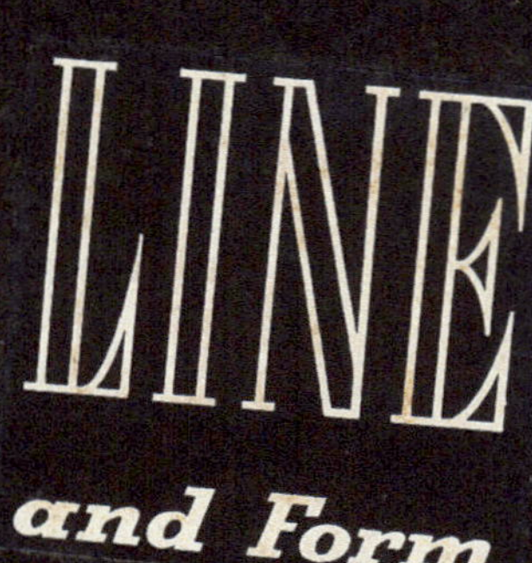

Name Merseyside Press

No.

9351.

Duplex tone (Yellow and Black)

Line and Form

Opposite: Printer's mechanical for the cover of *Line and Form* no. 4. The model is Stella Fabian (aka Veronique).

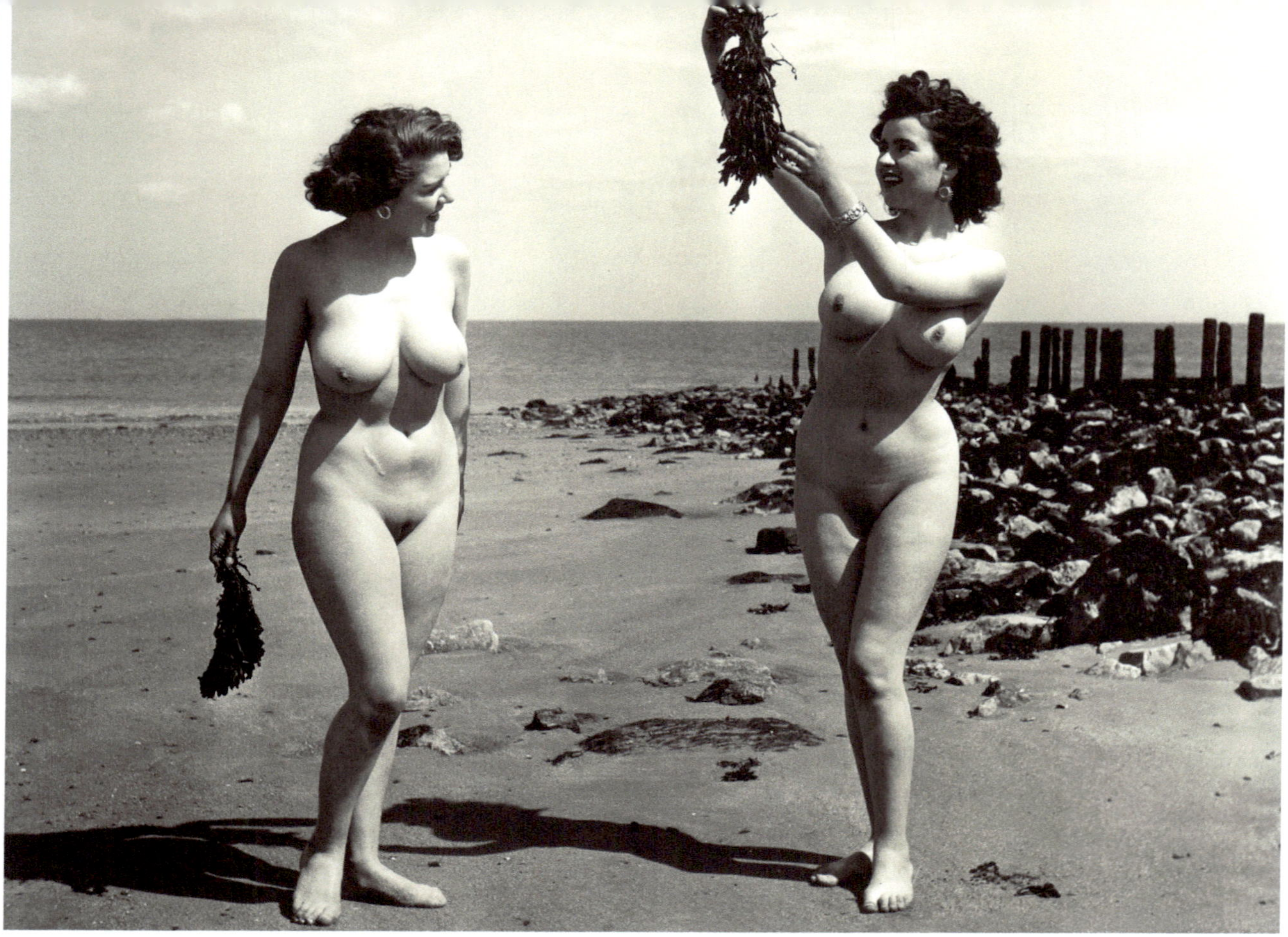

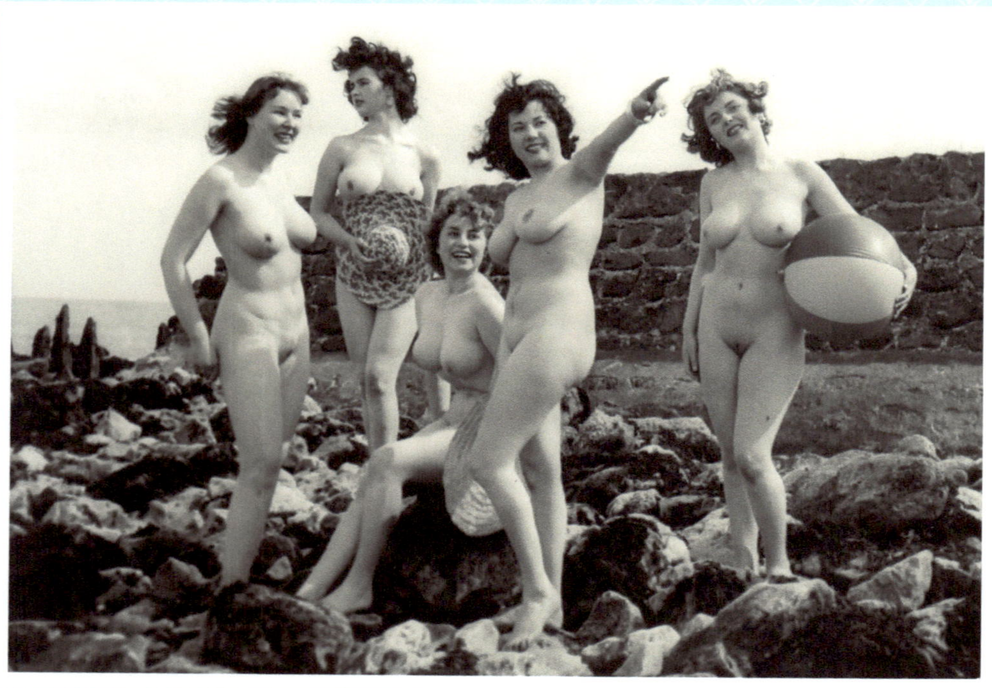

Left: Margaret, Kate, Valerie, Sylvana, Linda, 1956.

Opposite: The pneumatic Diane Du Bois.

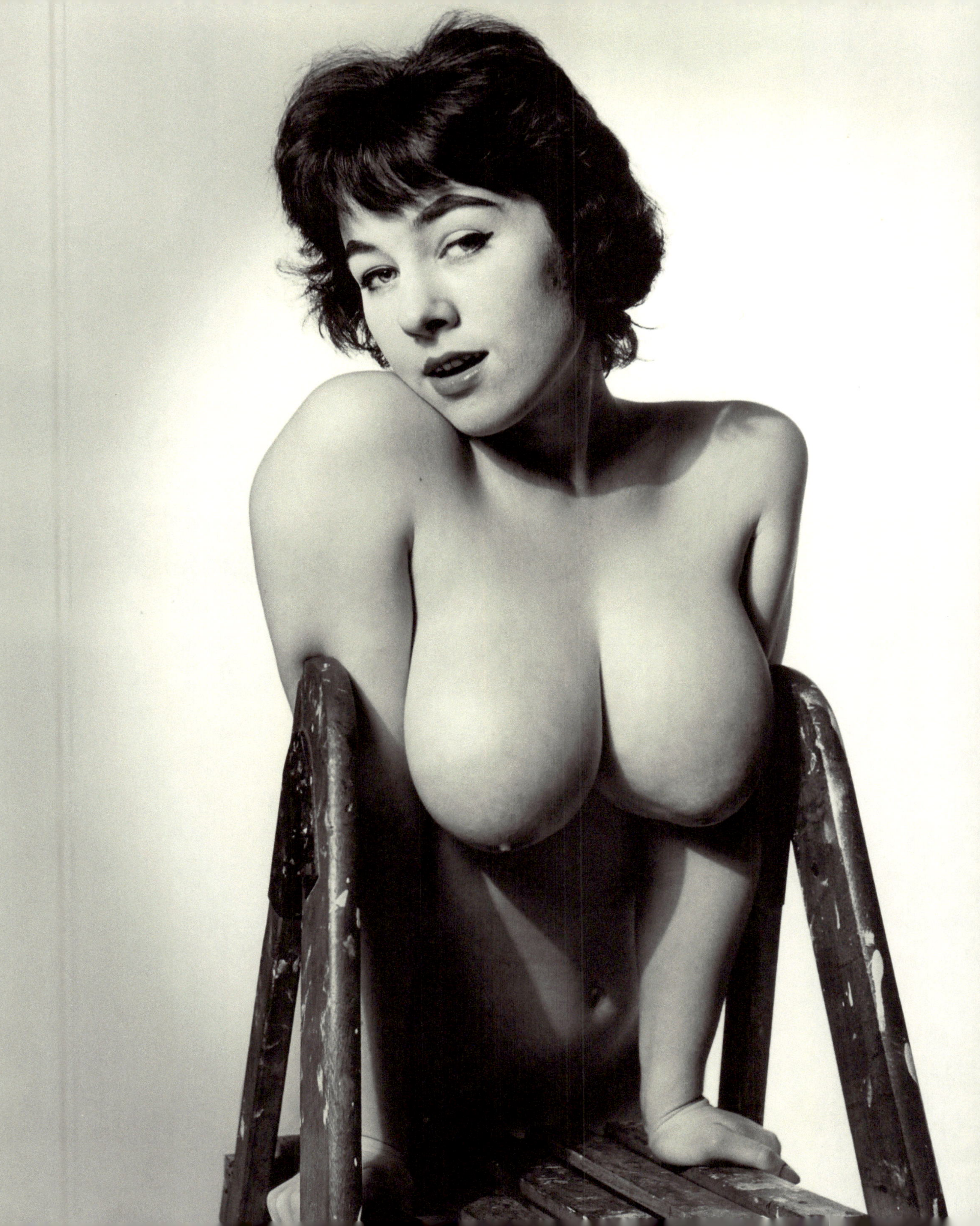

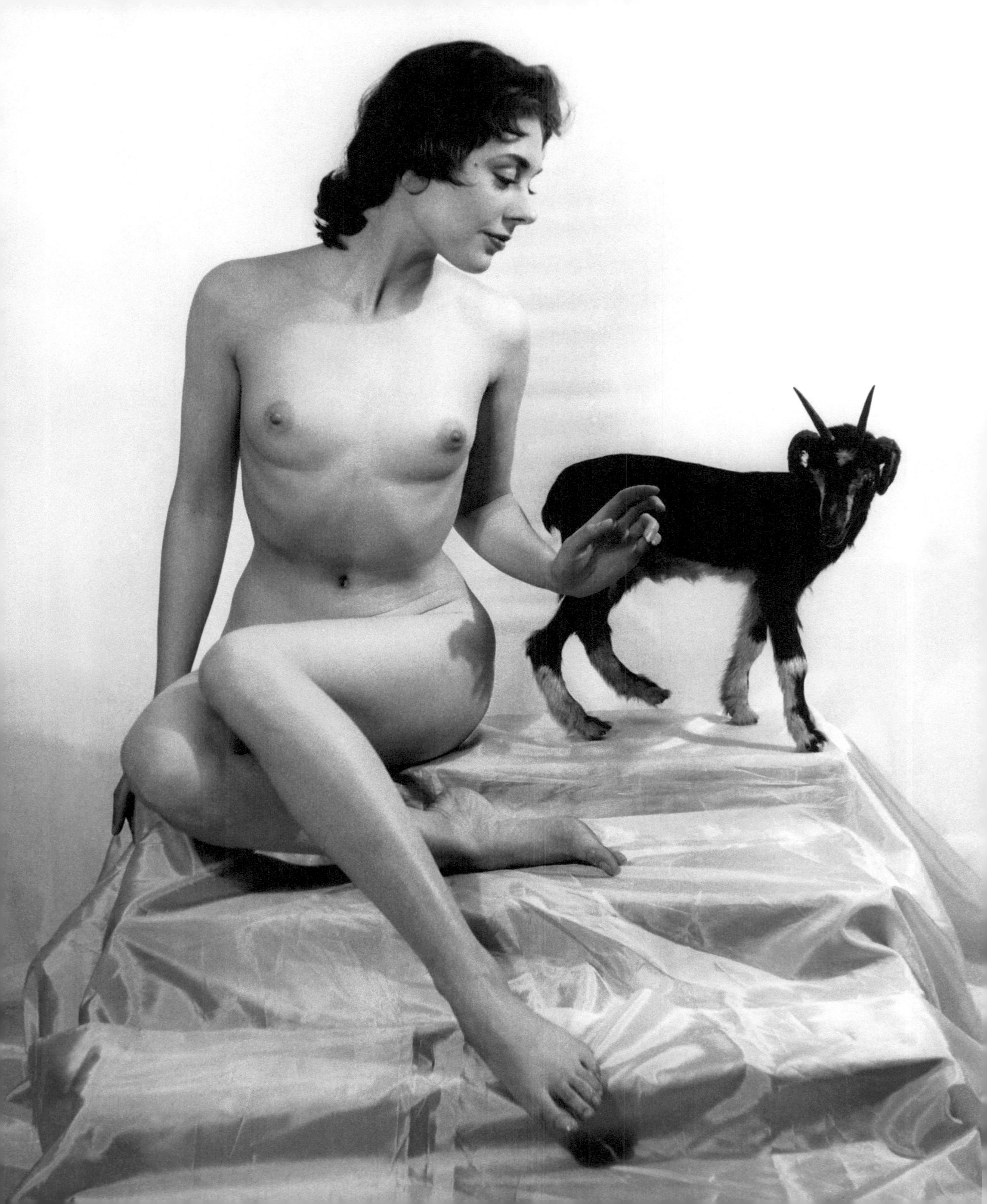

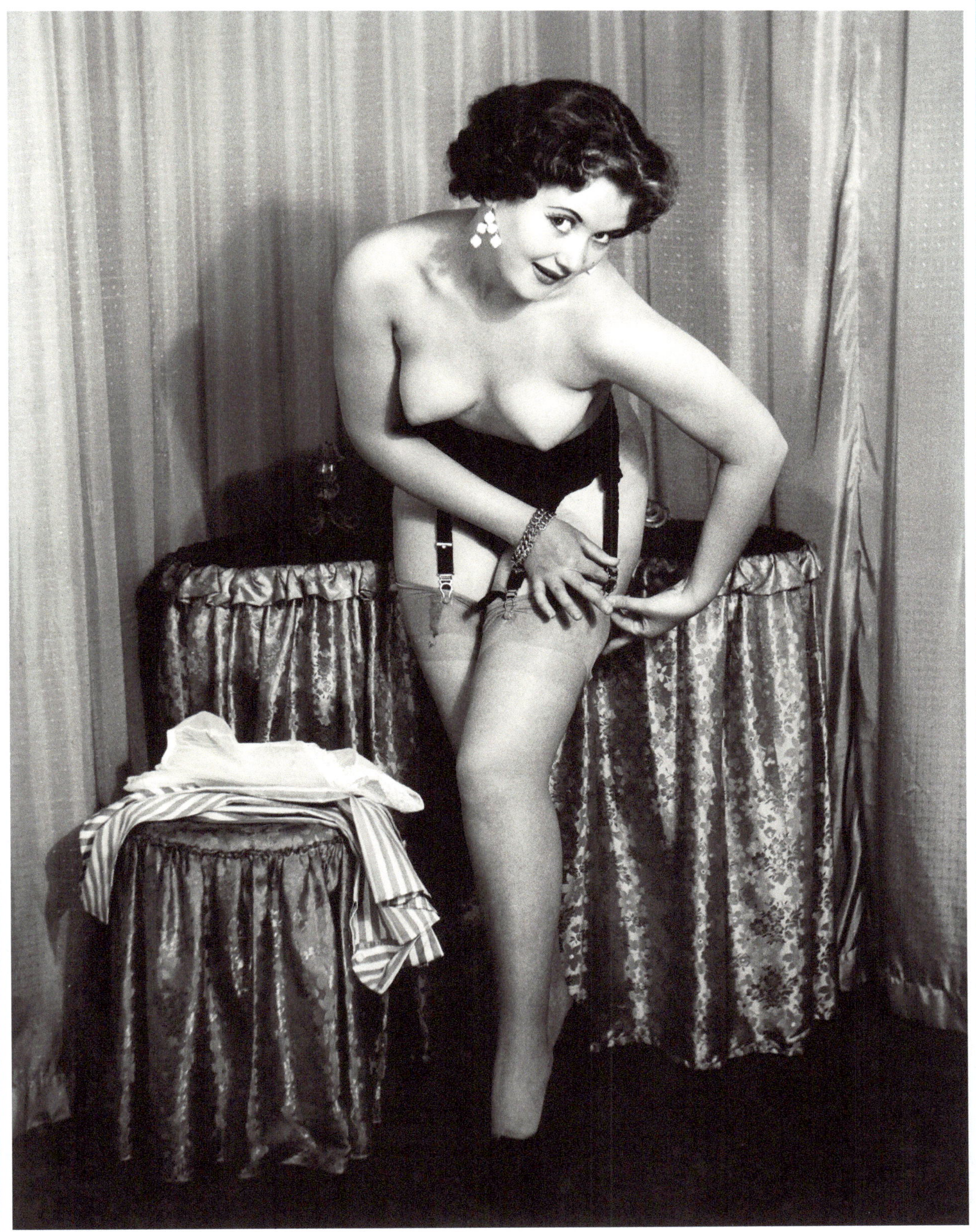

Above: Gloria Latham. **Opposite:** Mara Fox.

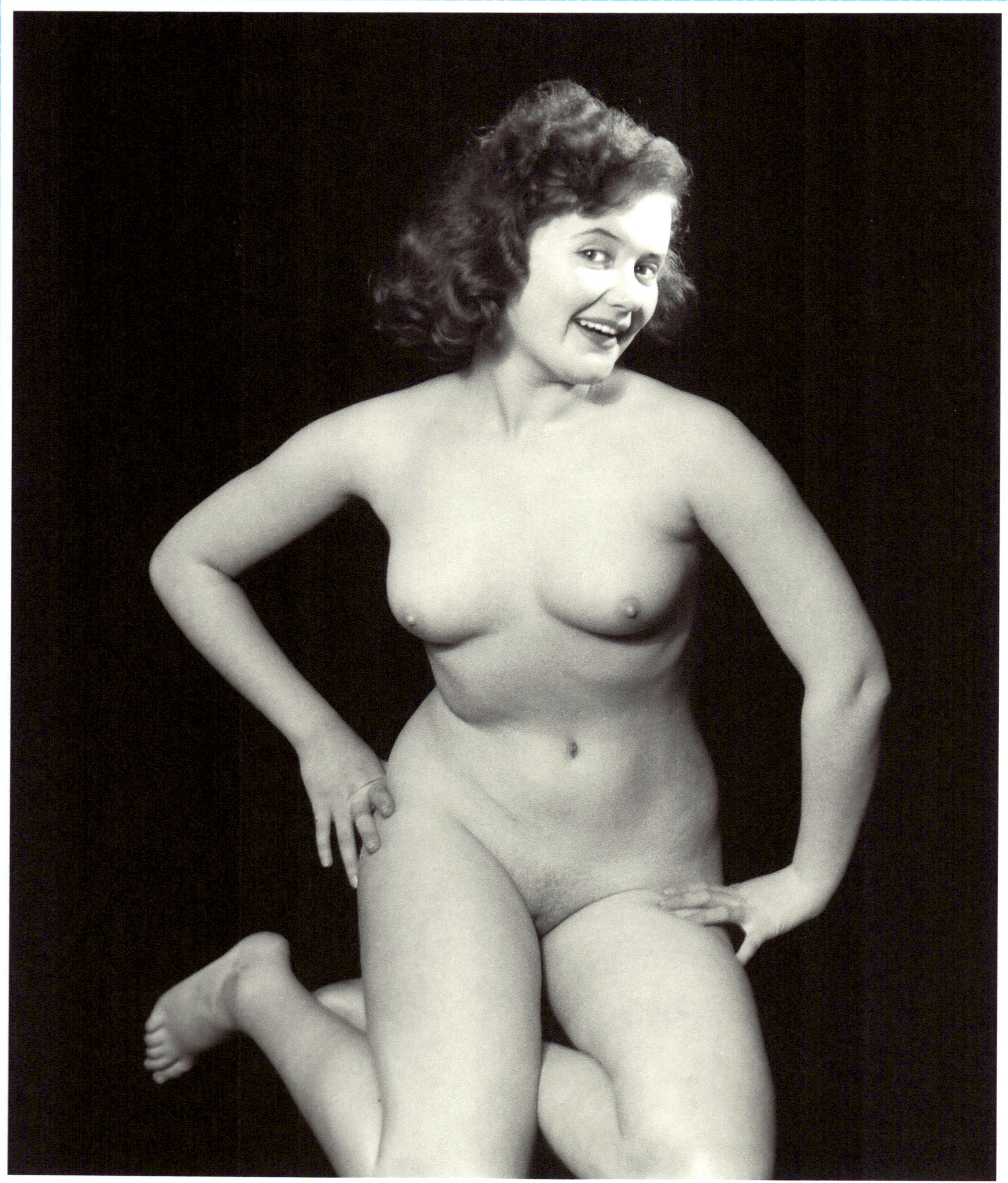

Above: Gloria Latham.

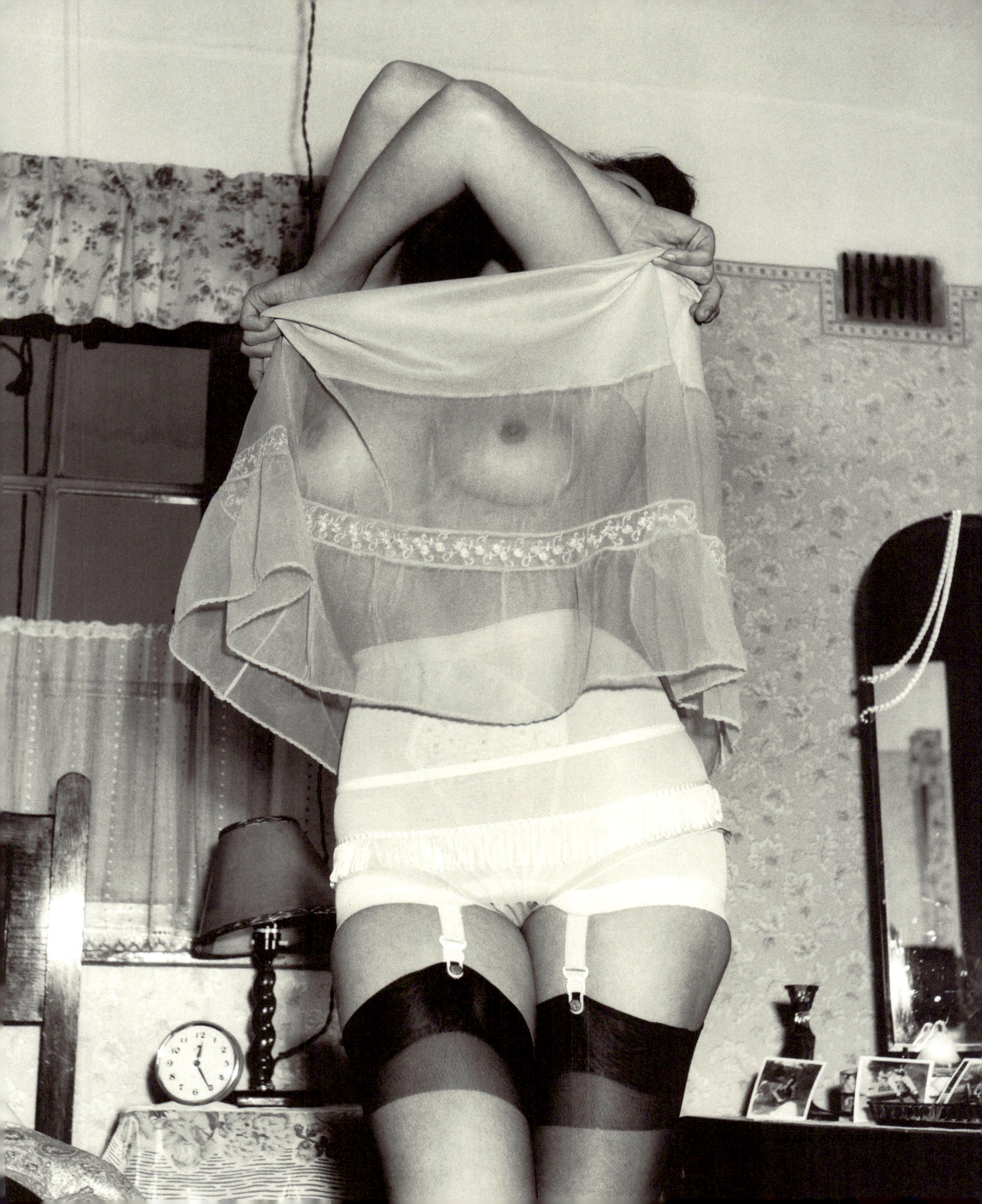

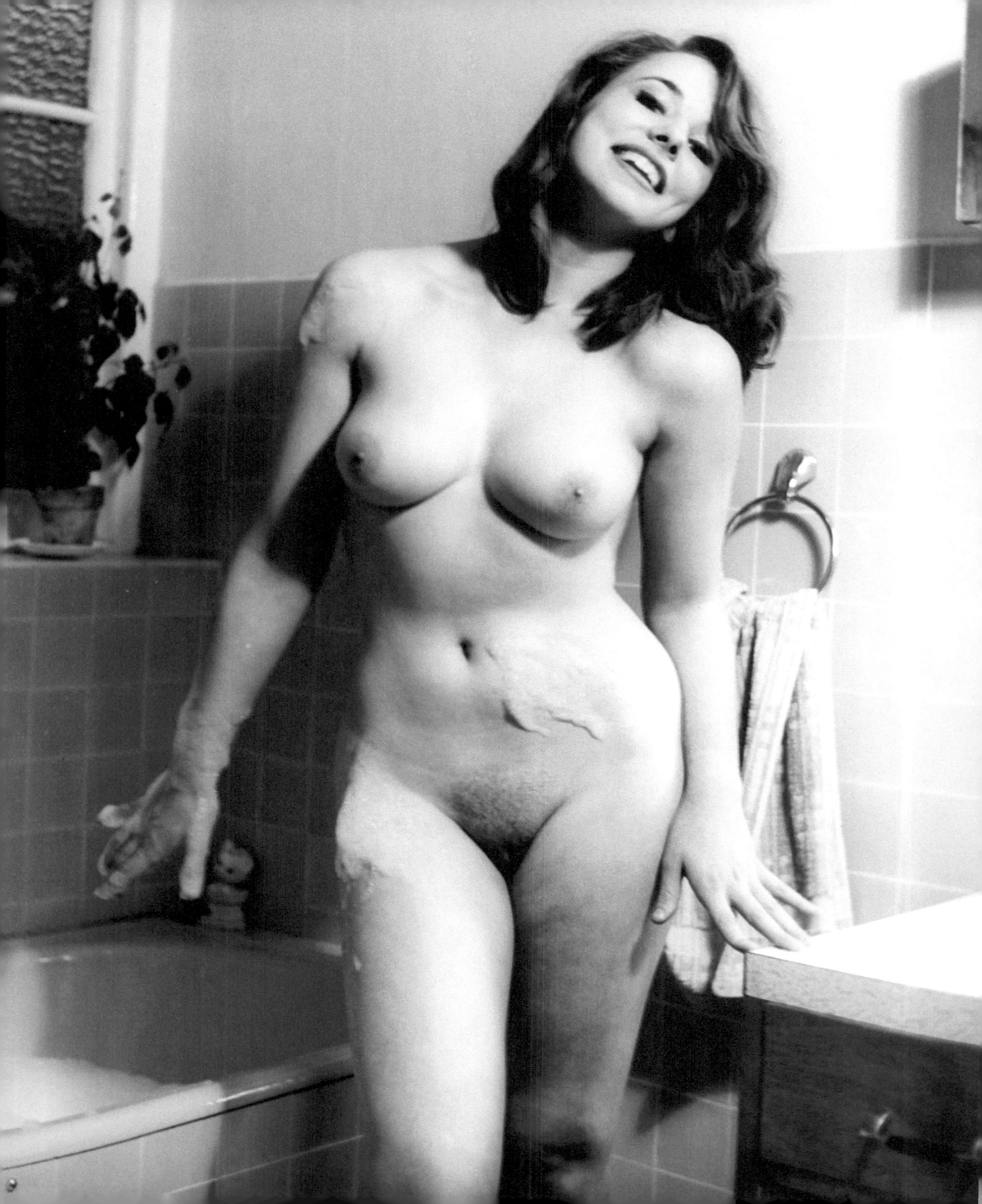

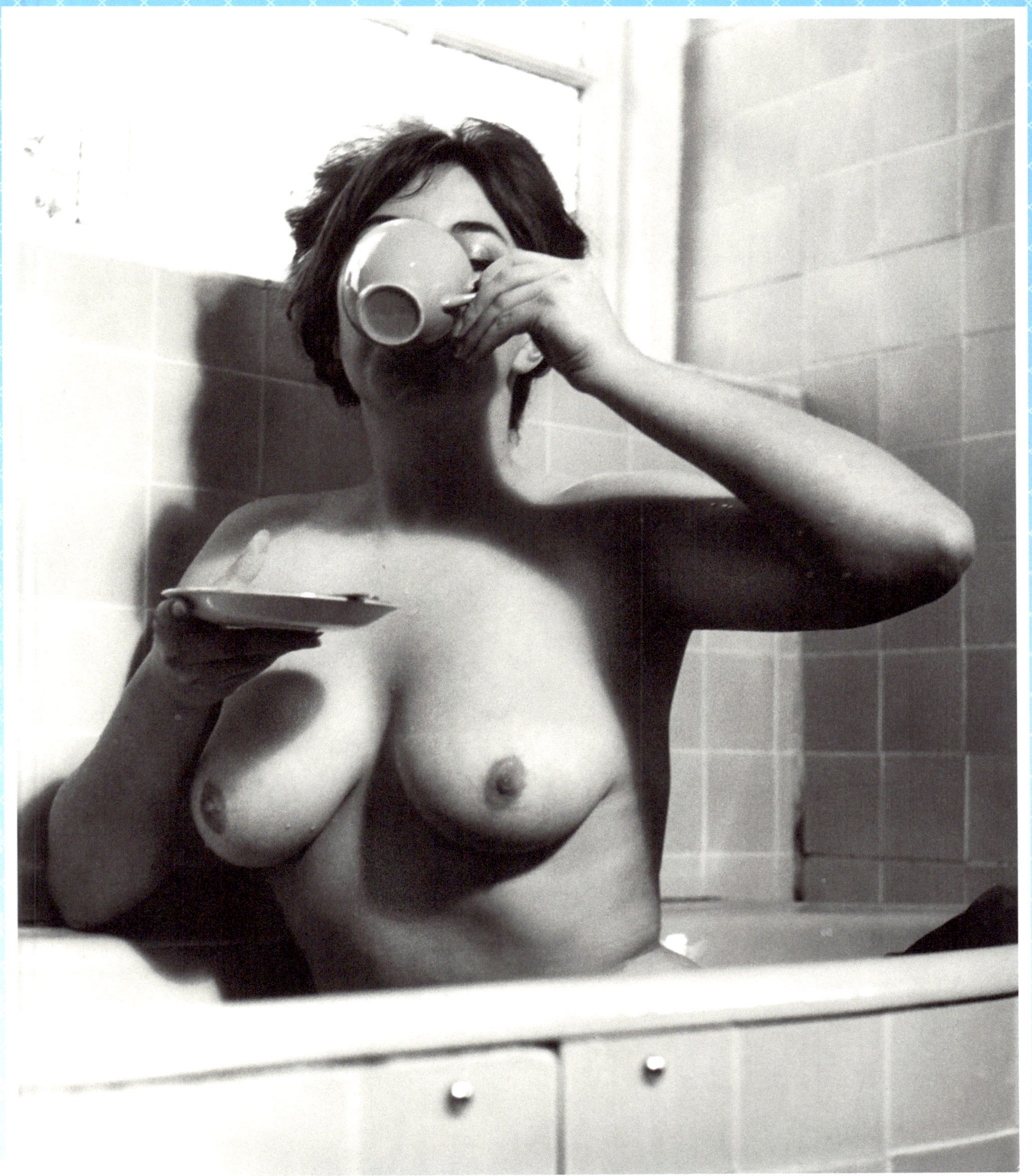

Above: Valerie Smith. **Opposite:** Barbara Raynham.

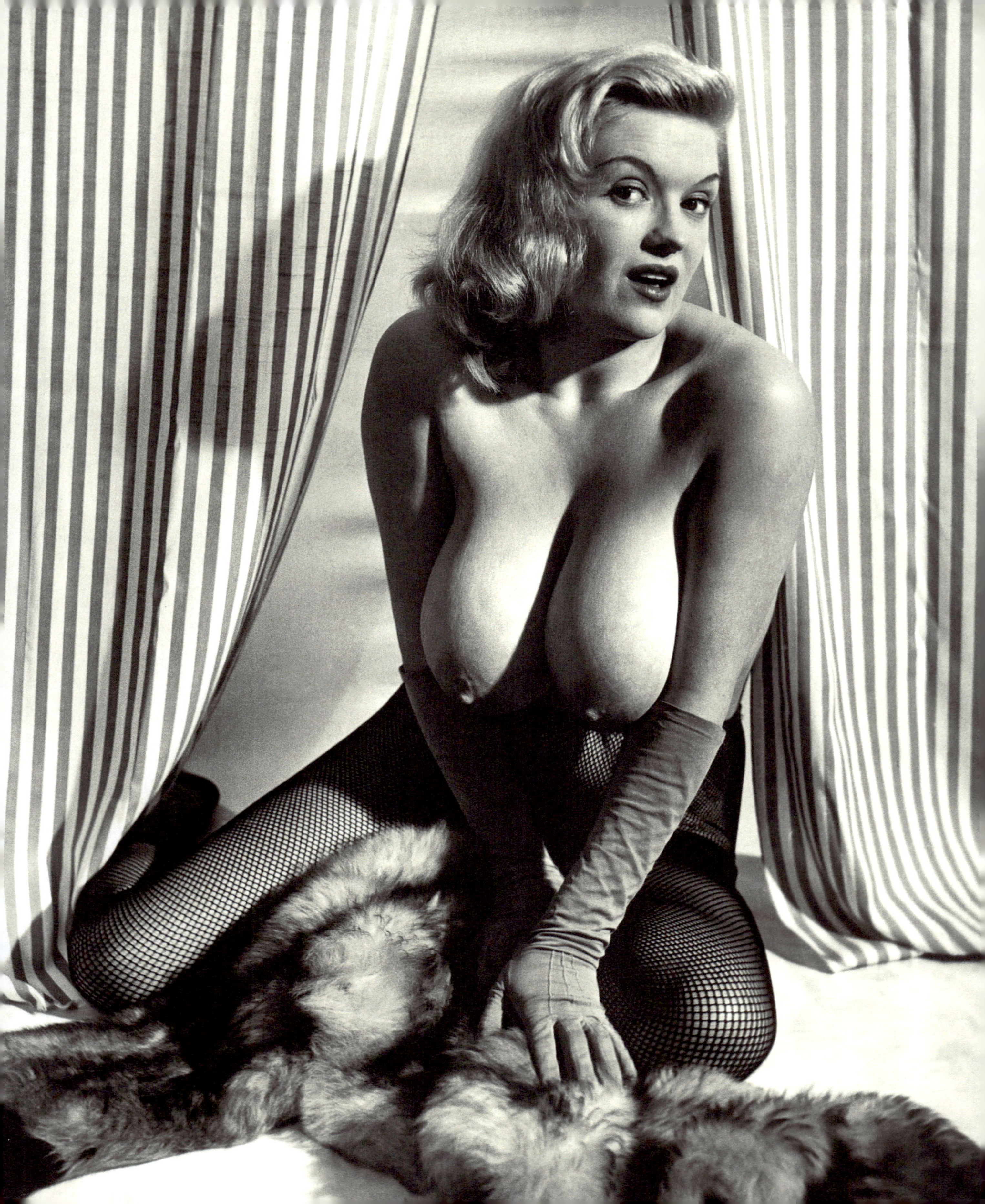

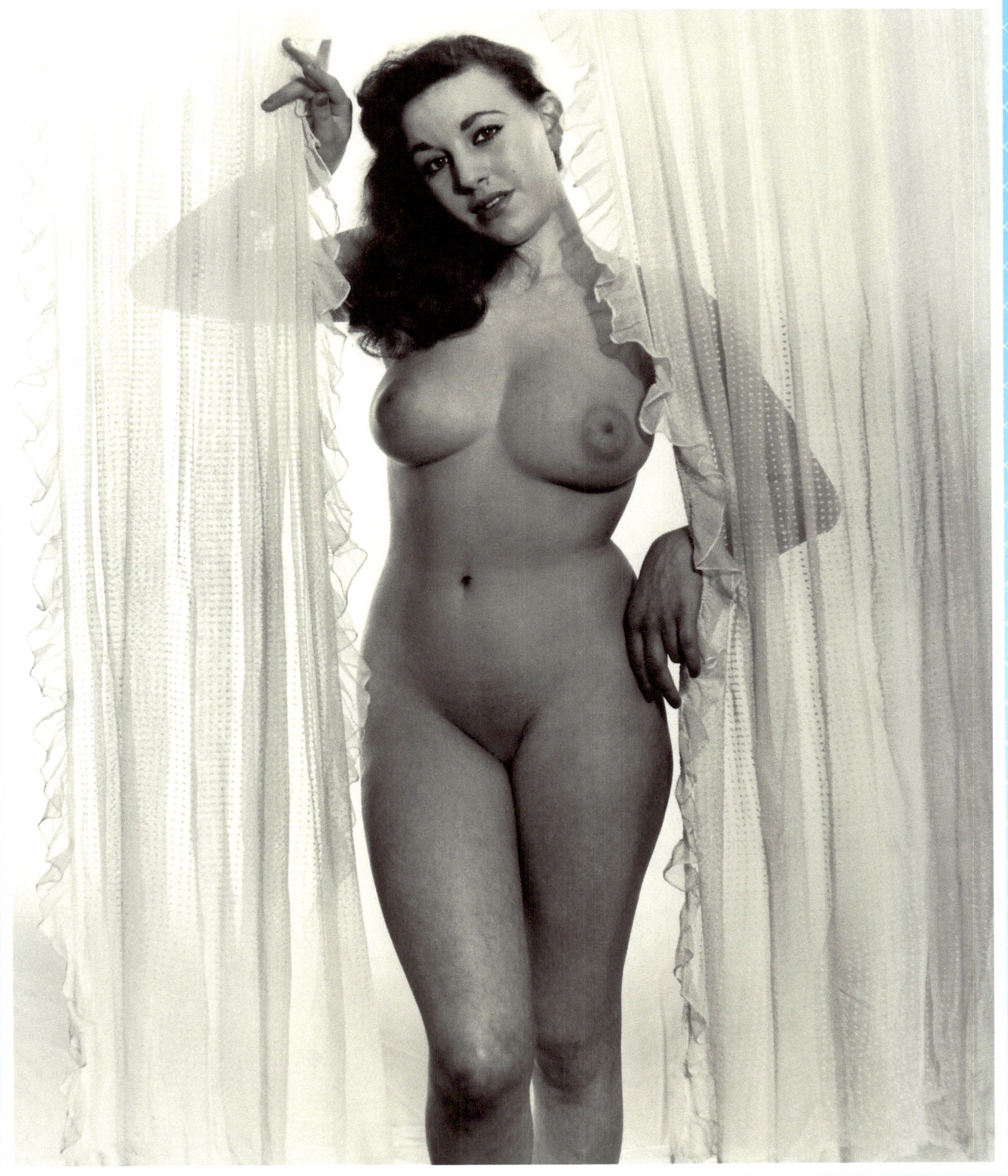

Above: Della Fox. **Opposite:** Paula Page and her bountiful breasts.

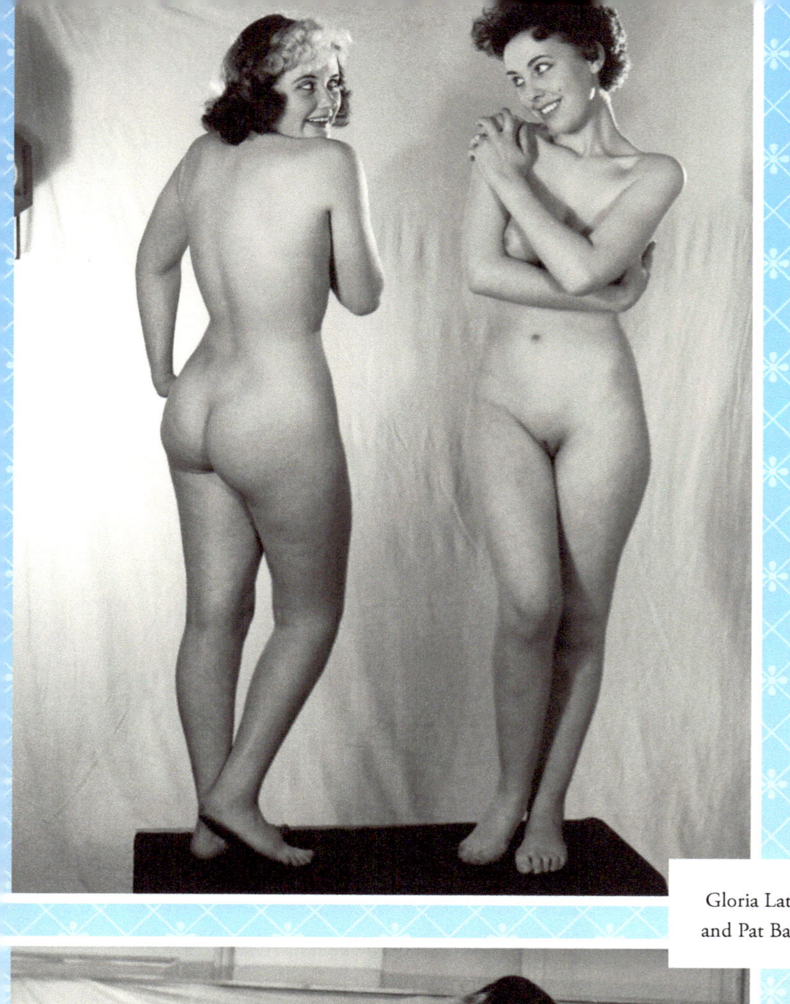
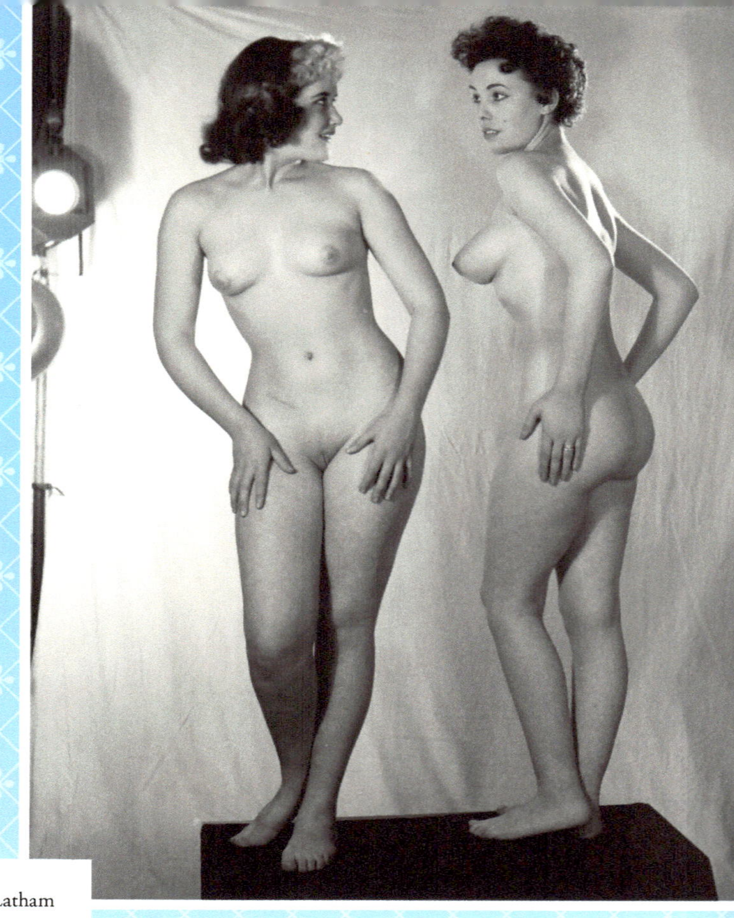
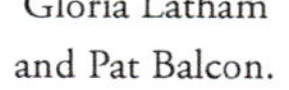

Gloria Latham
and Pat Balcon.

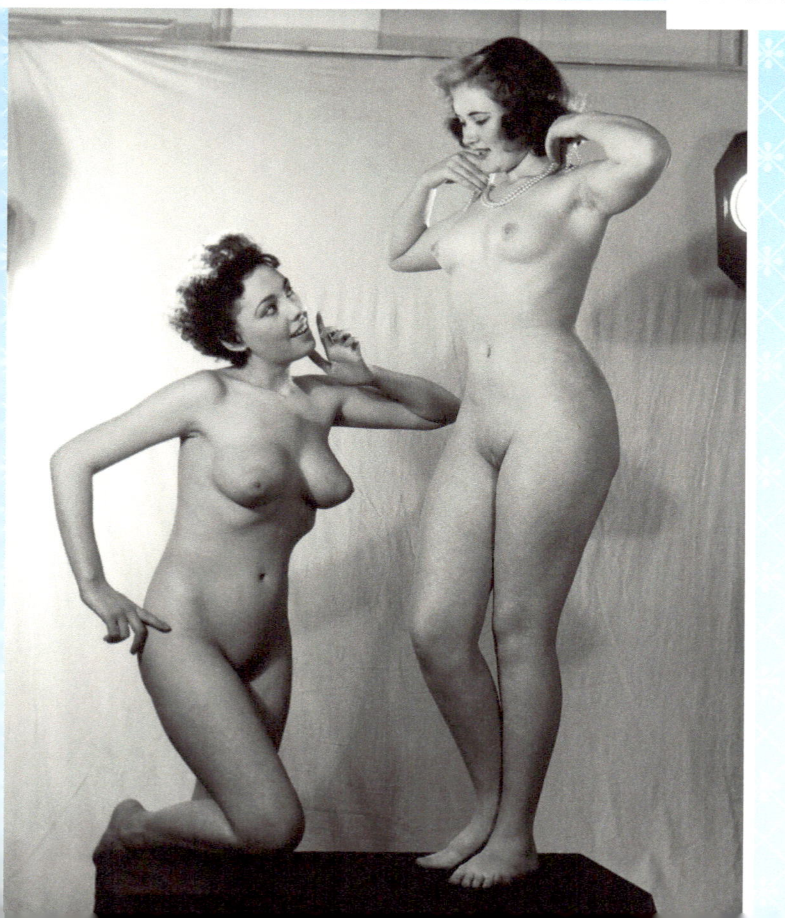
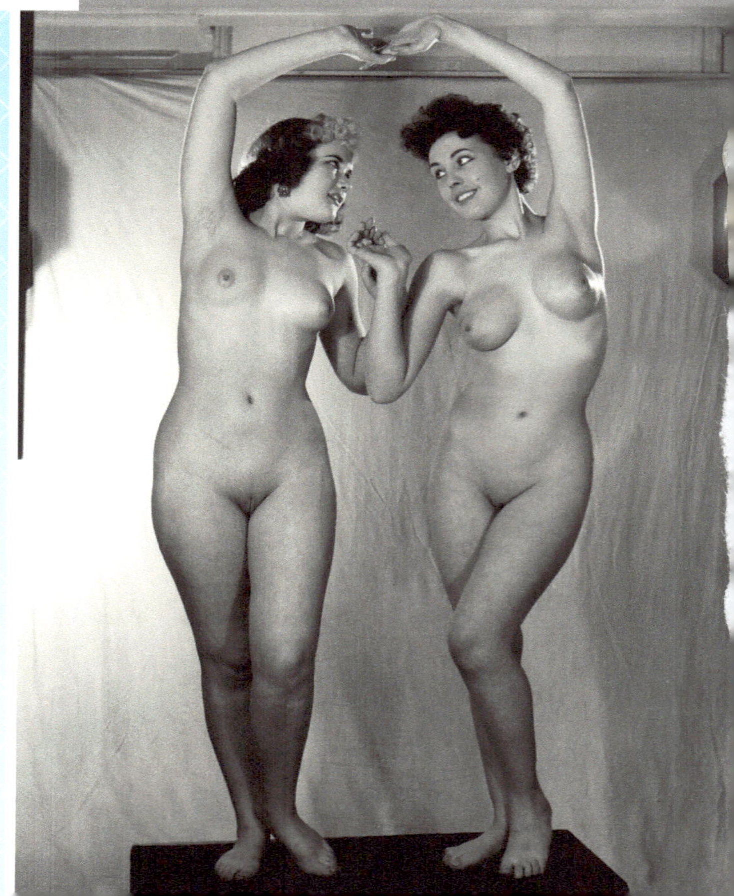

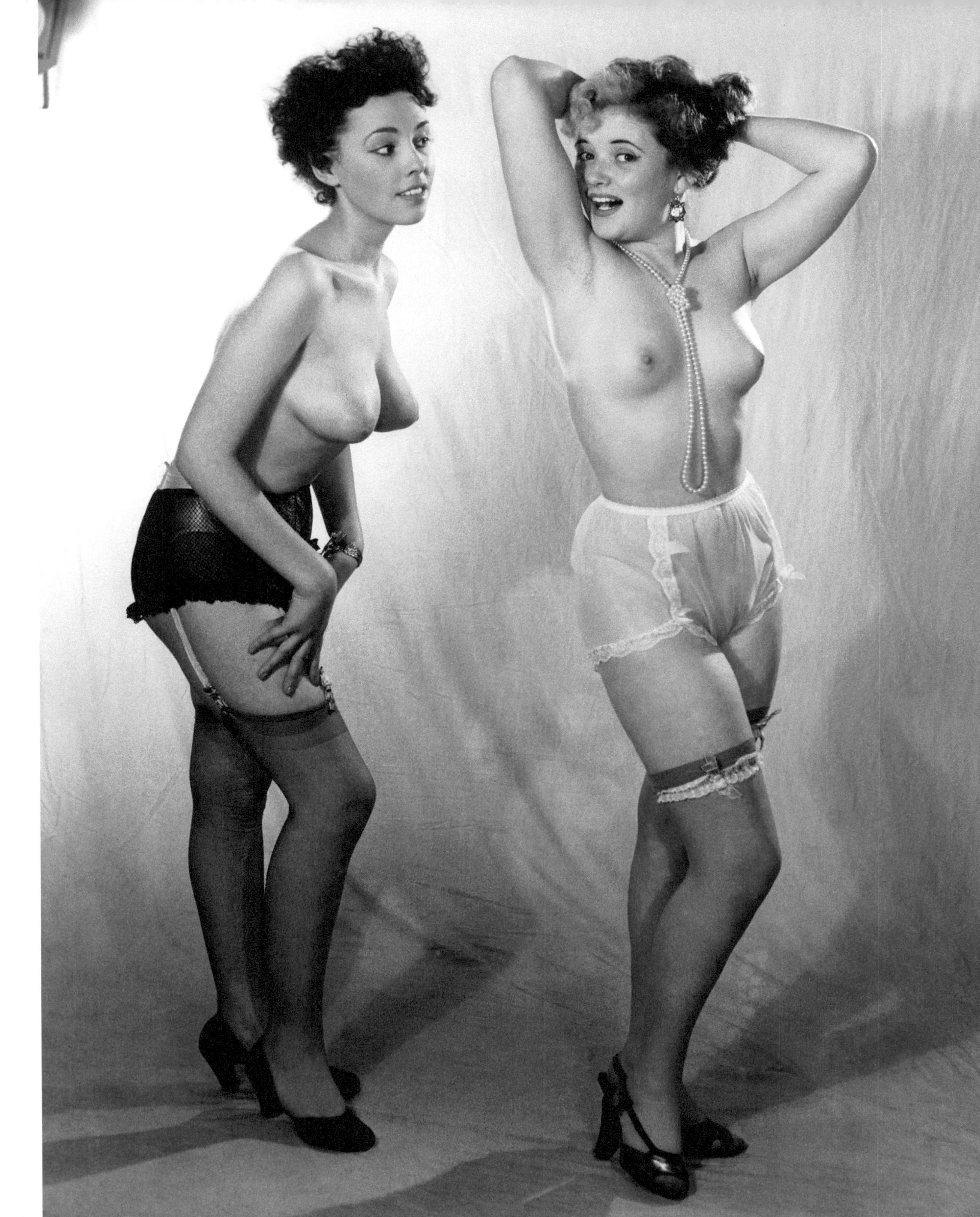

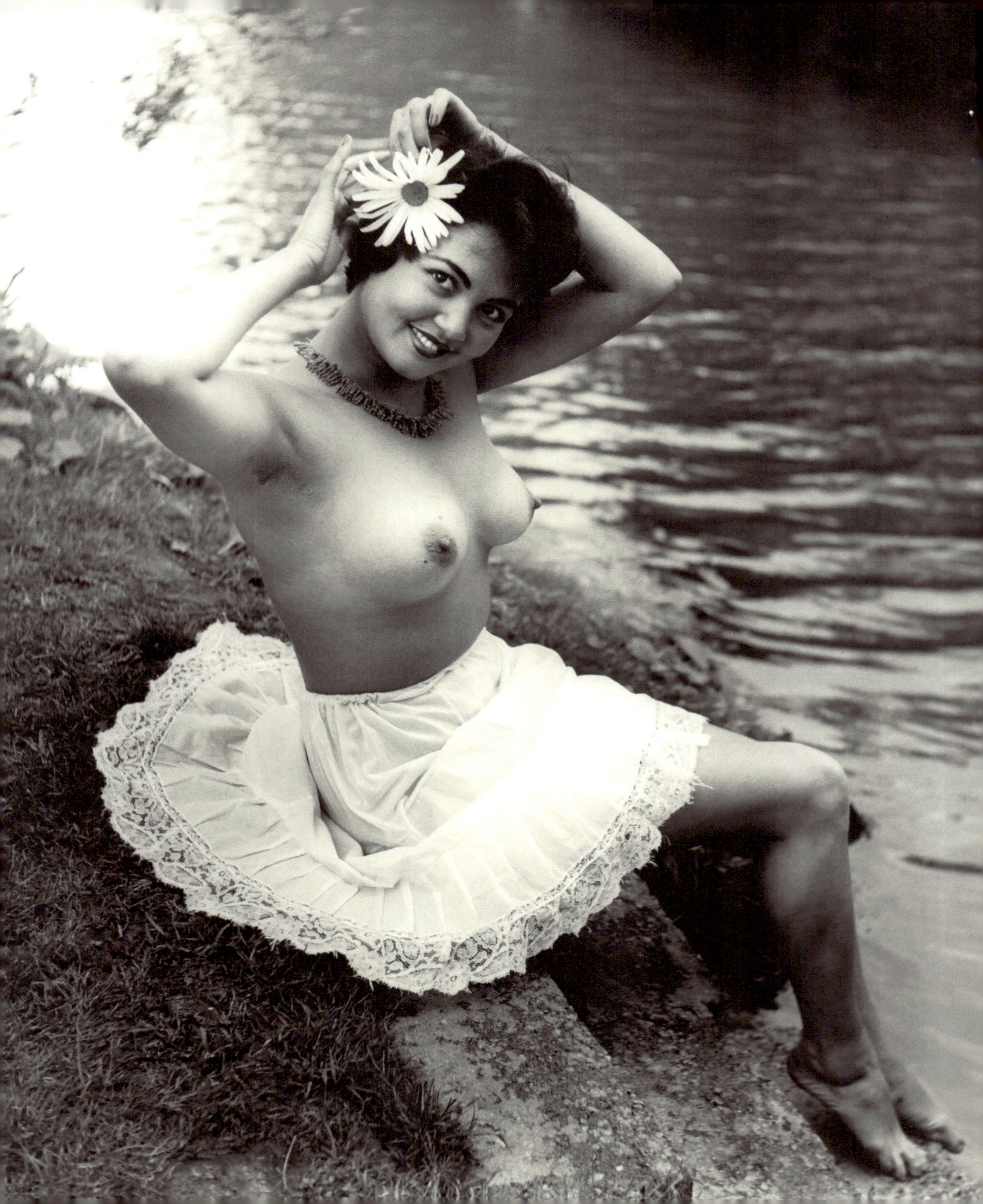

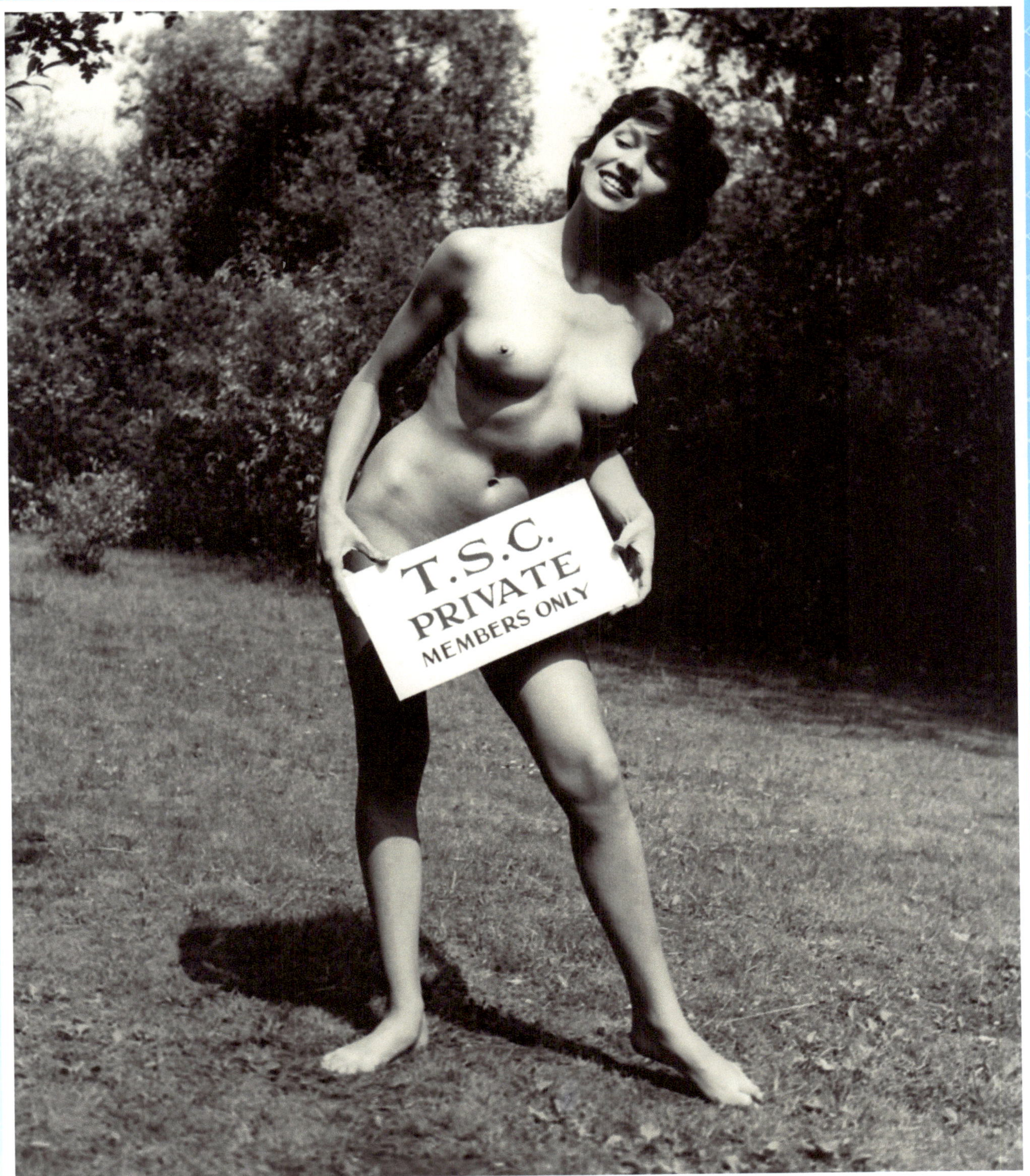

Above: Karen Stirling holding a sign for Thames Sun Club, the premises of which was a beautiful little island near Sunbury-on-Thames in Surrey.
Opposite: An intriguing mixture of East and West is seen in the sultry beauty of Crystal Dawson: she is part Malay, part Burmese, and part English.

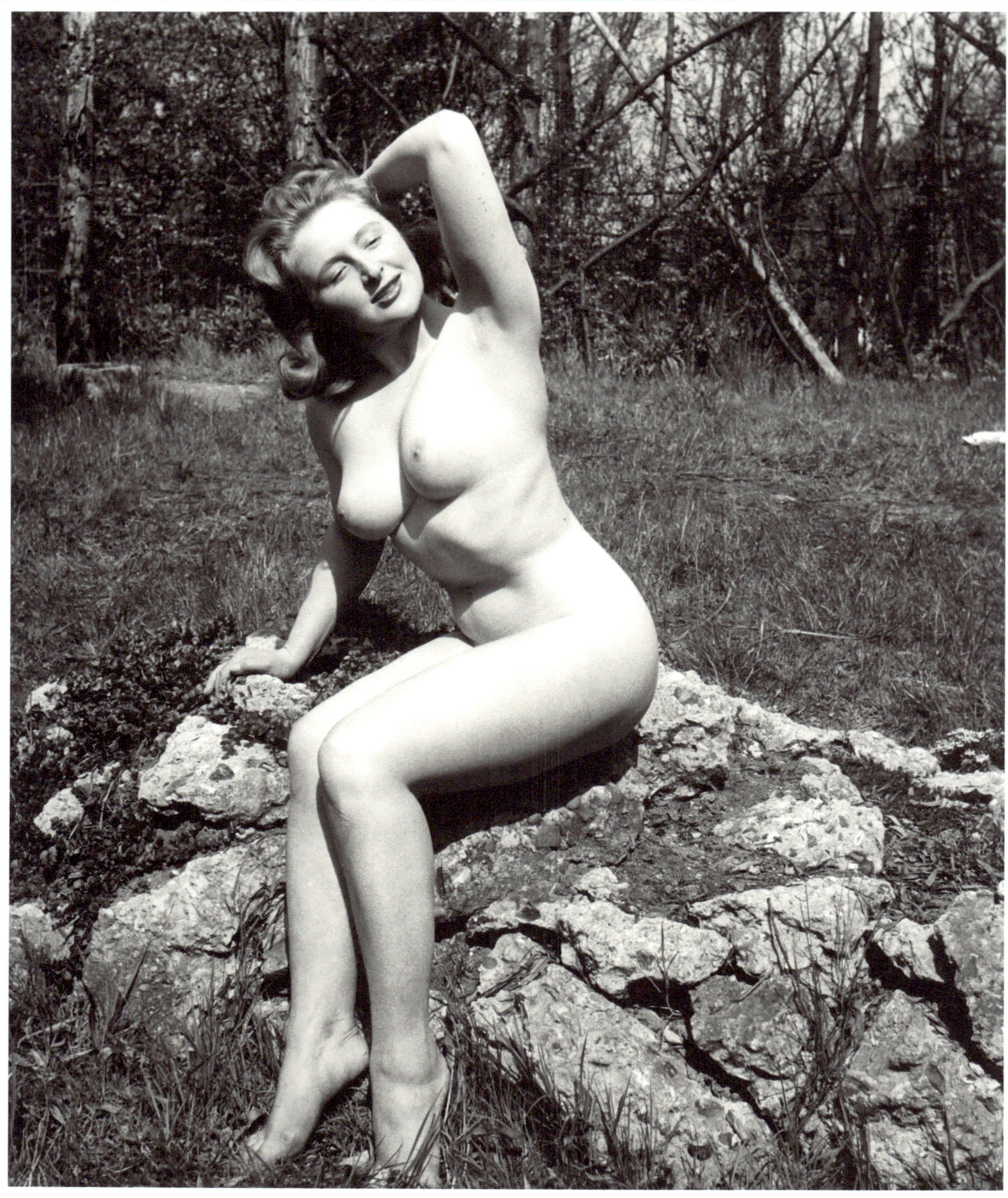

Above and opposite: Norma Forrest.

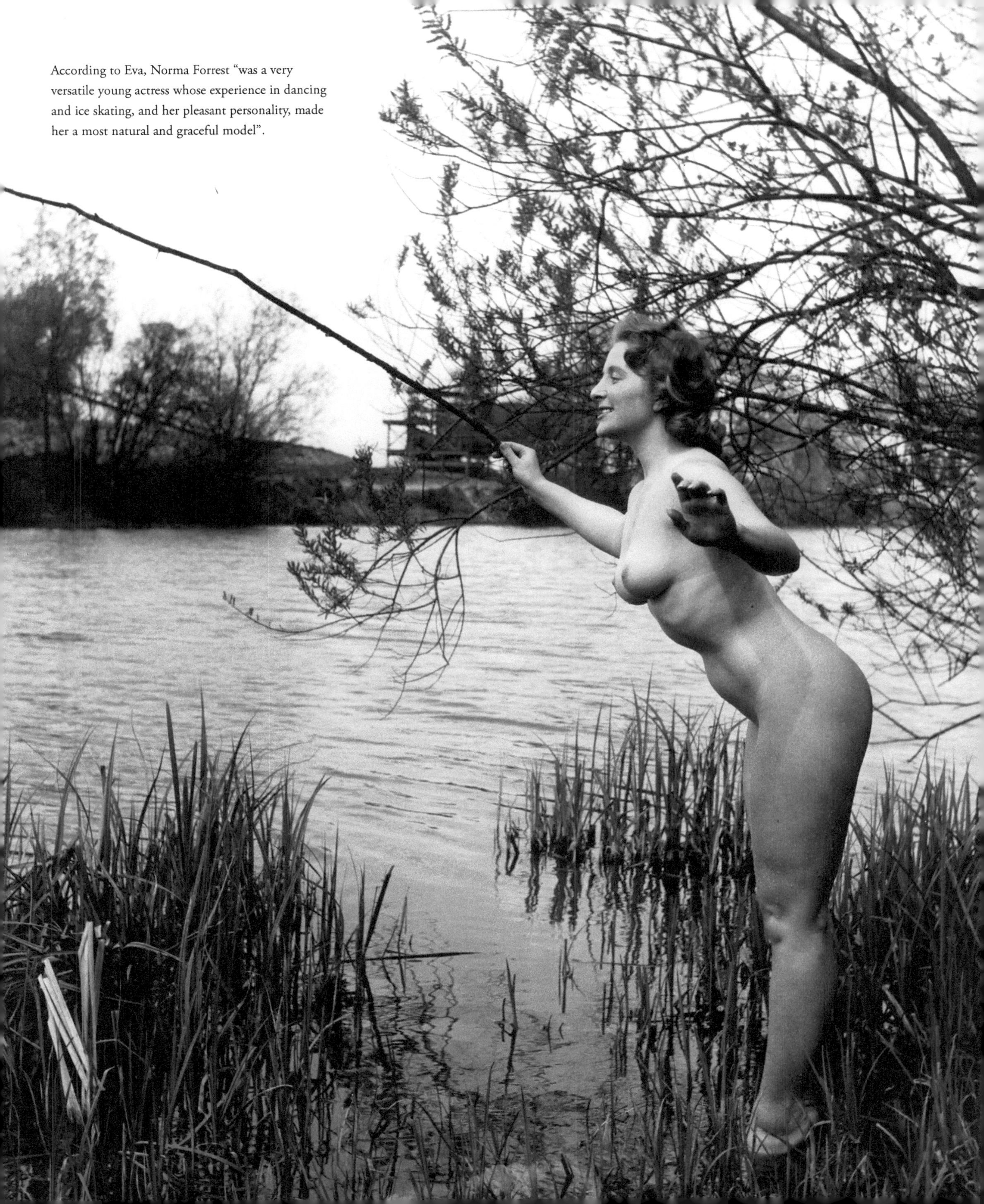

According to Eva, Norma Forrest "was a very versatile young actress whose experience in dancing and ice skating, and her pleasant personality, made her a most natural and graceful model".

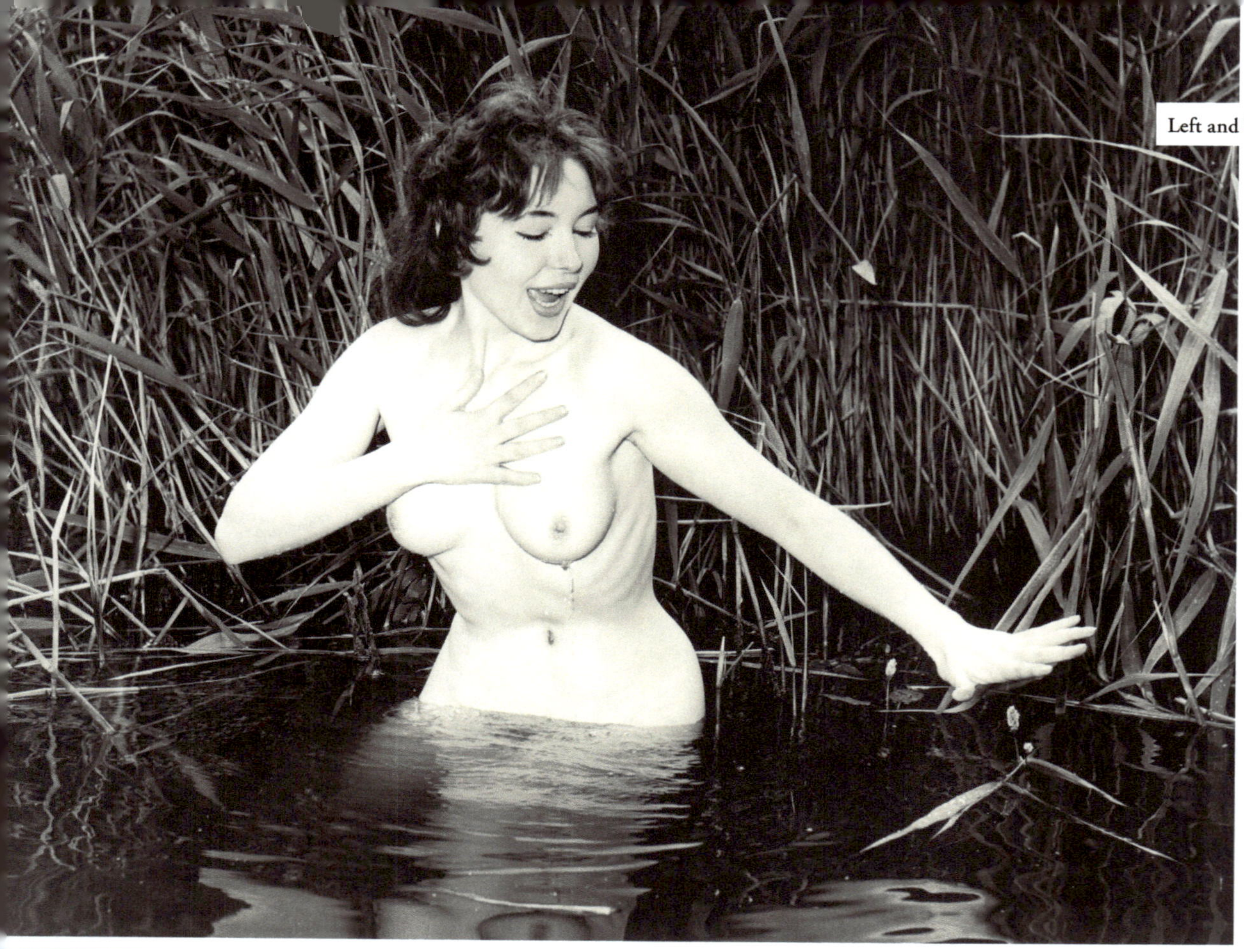

Left and below: Sally Ann Scott.

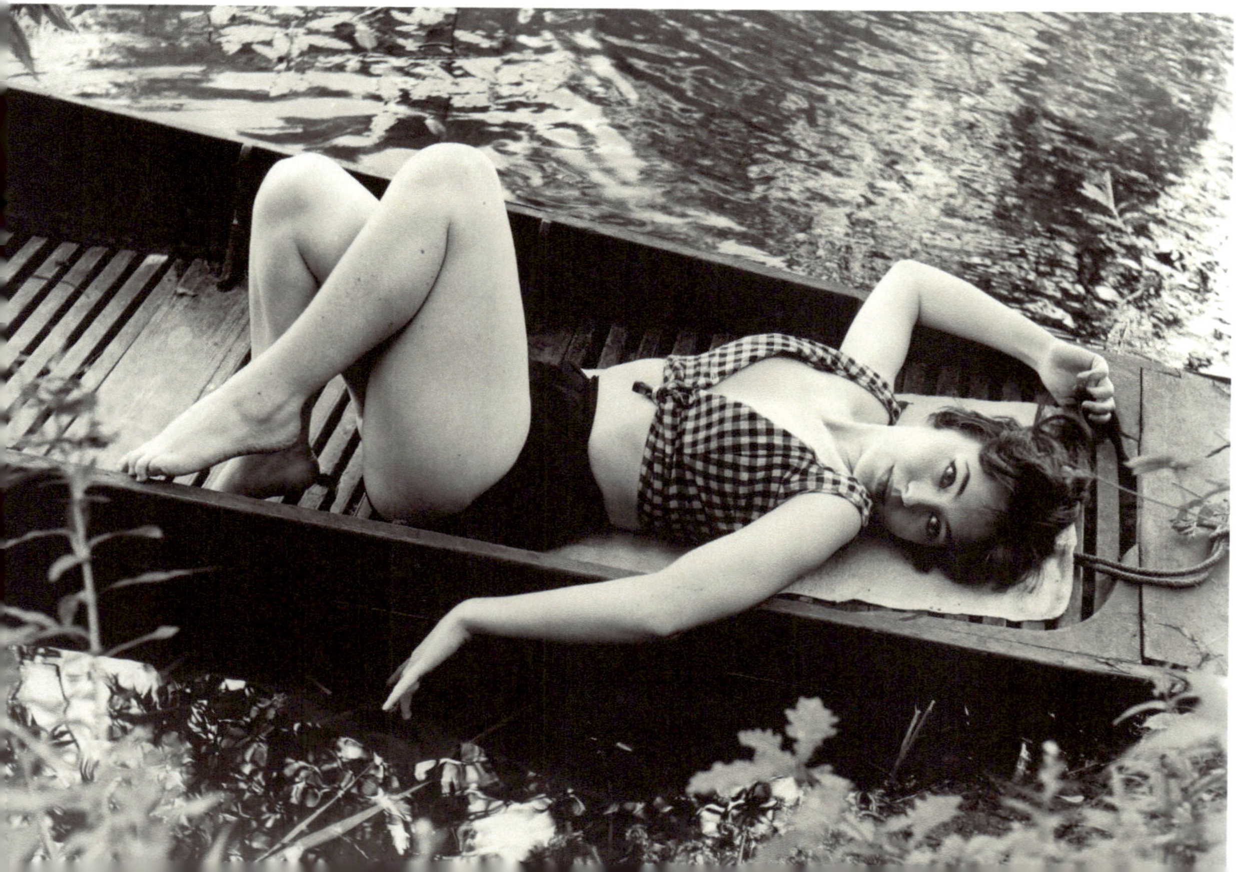

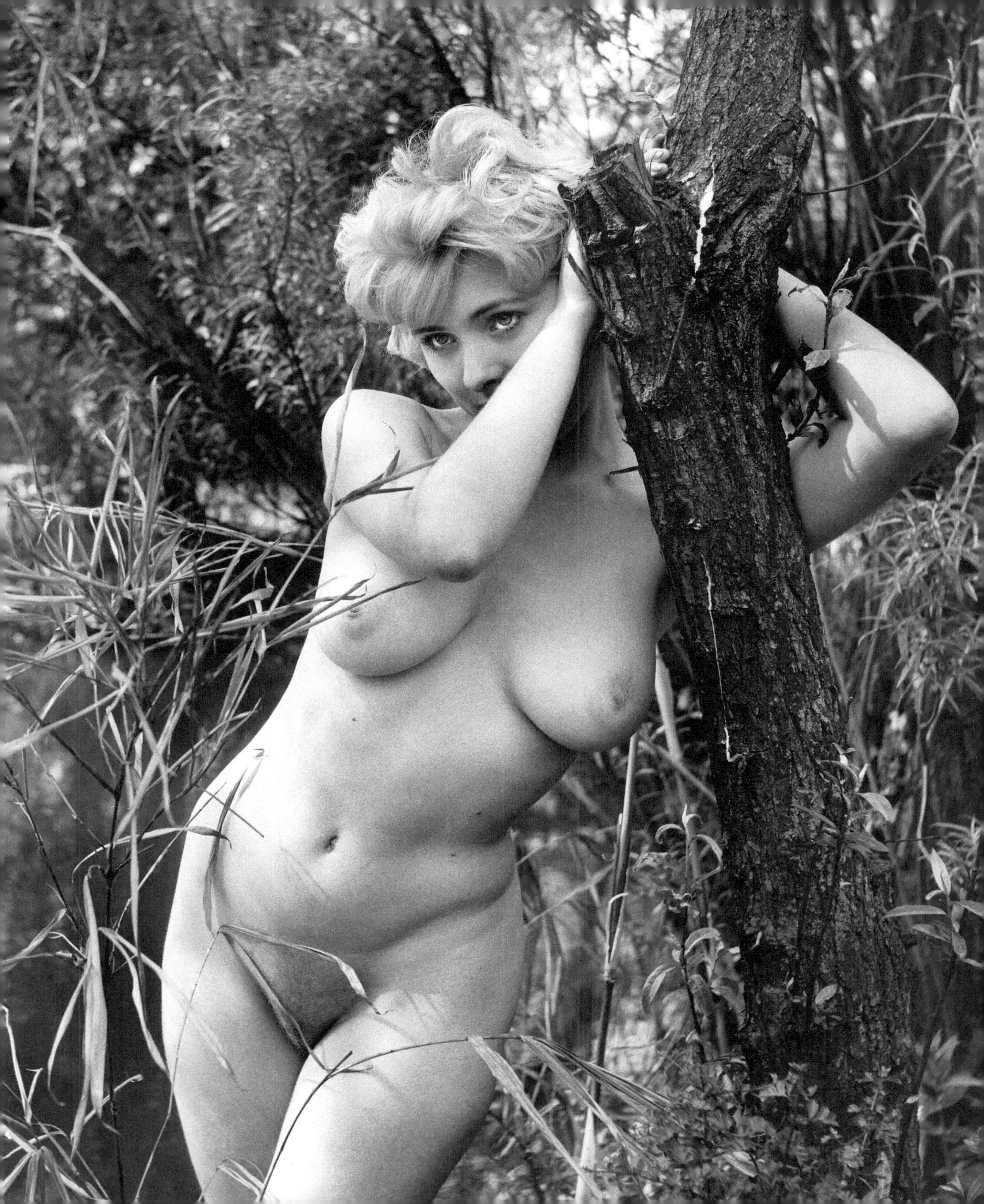

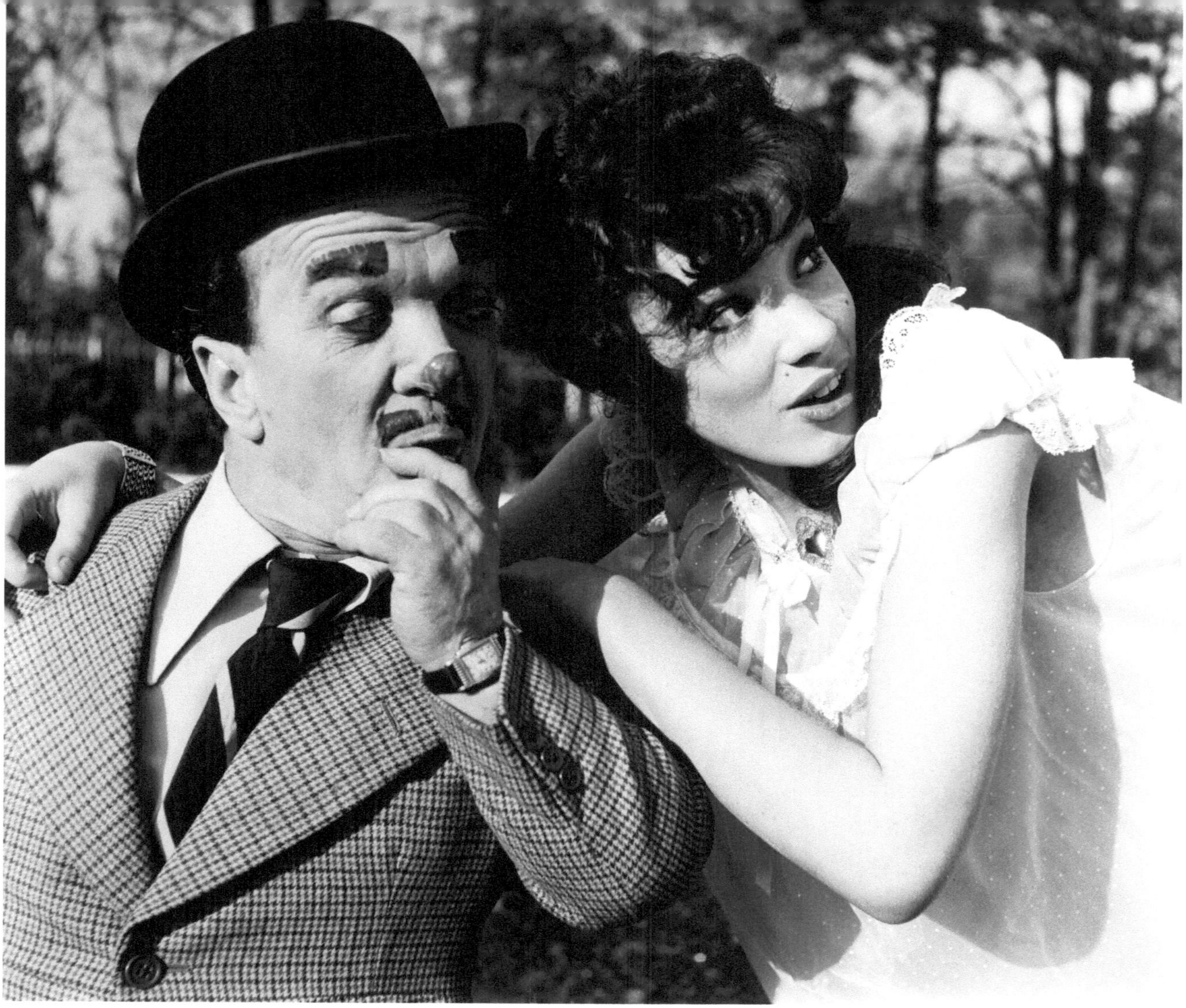

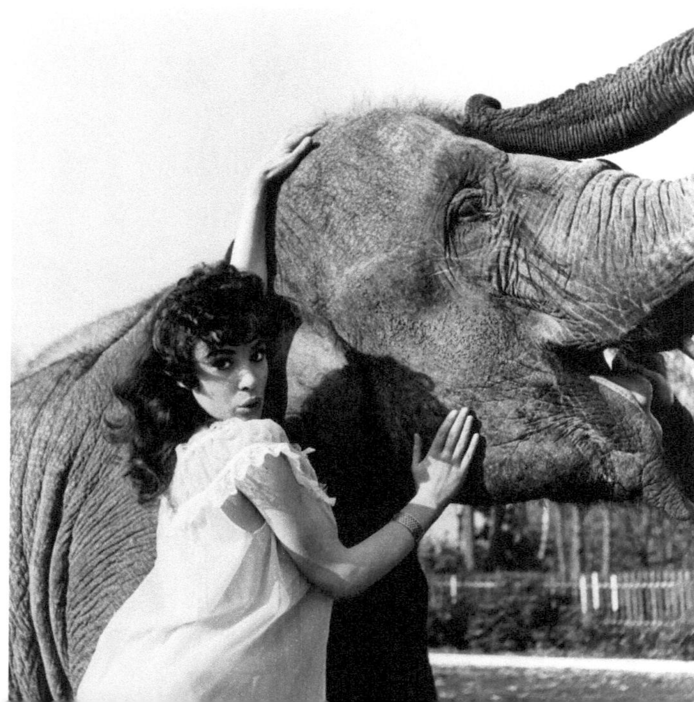
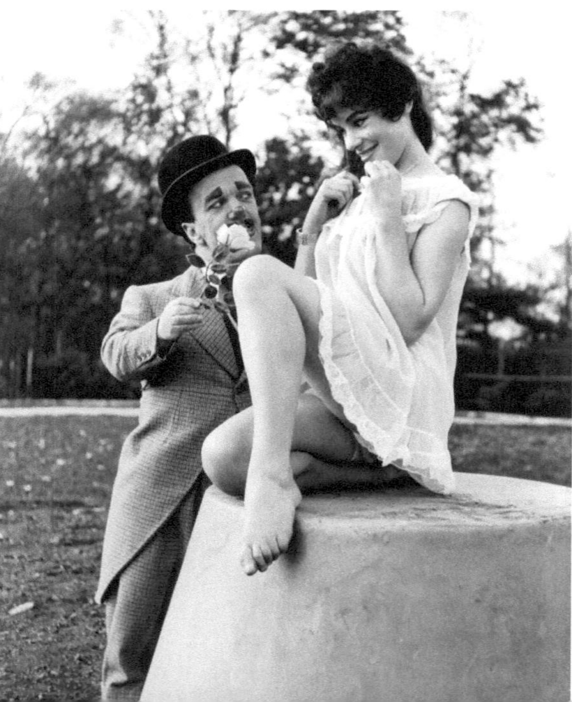

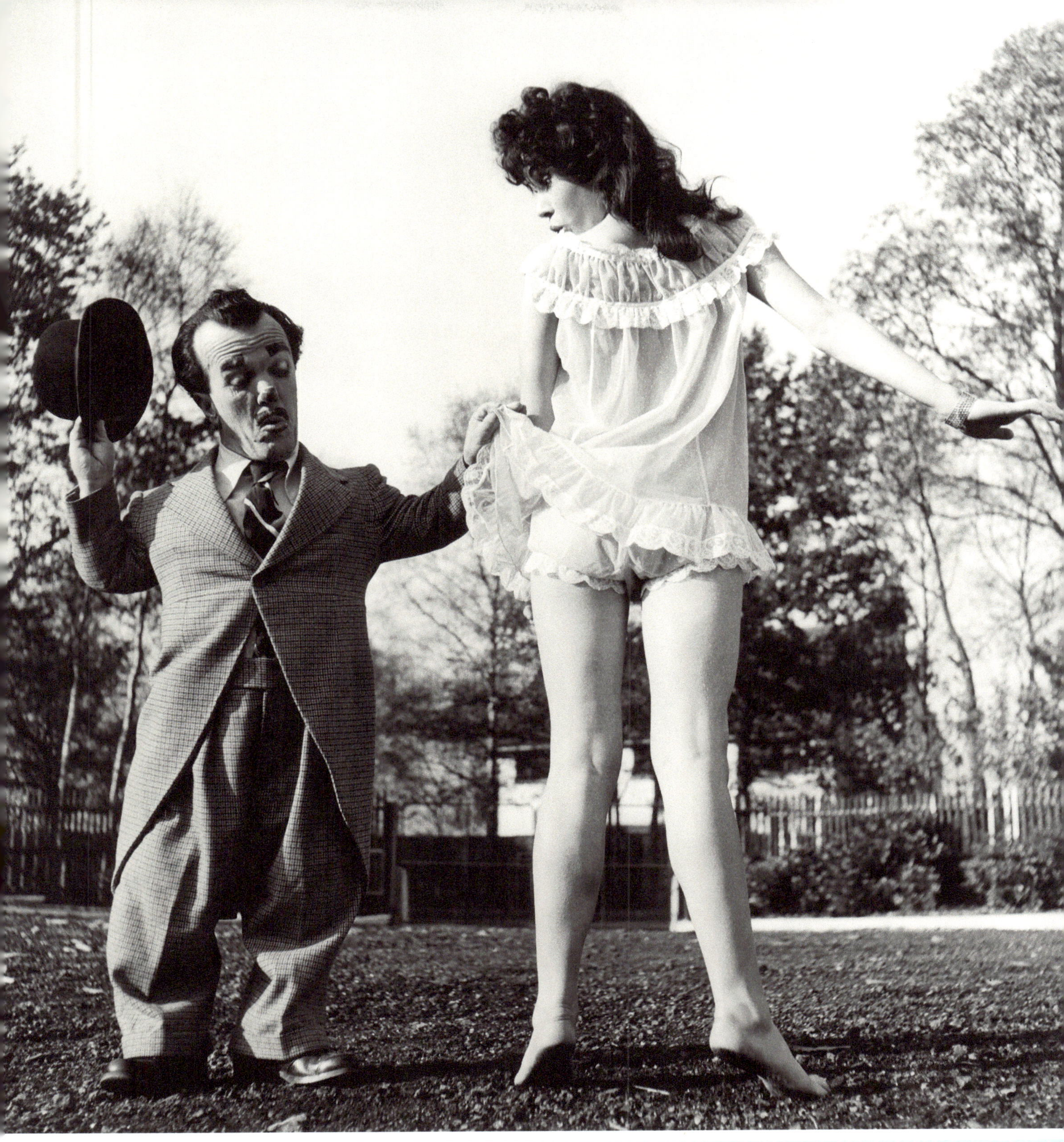

Above and opposite: Anita Baldrey.

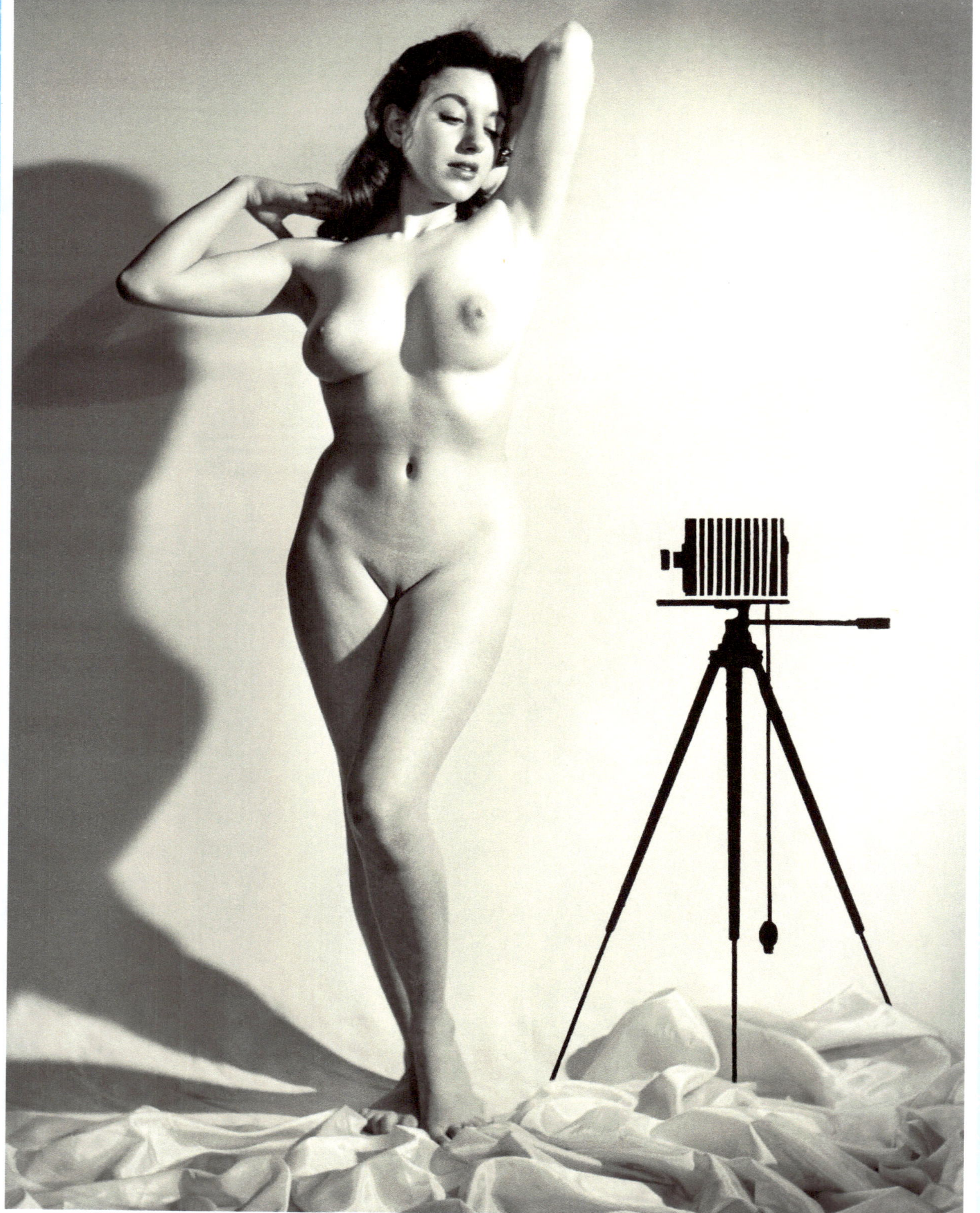

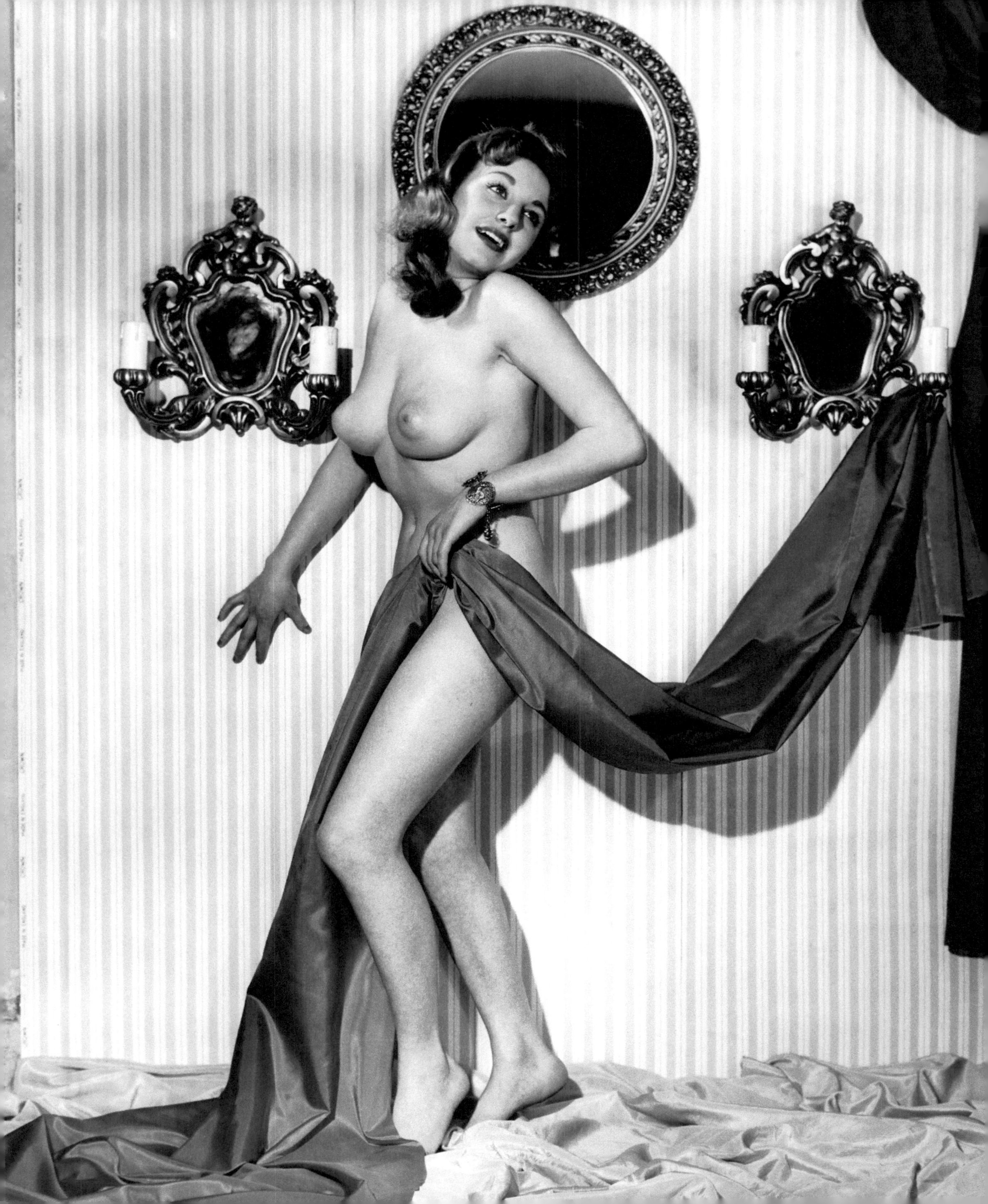

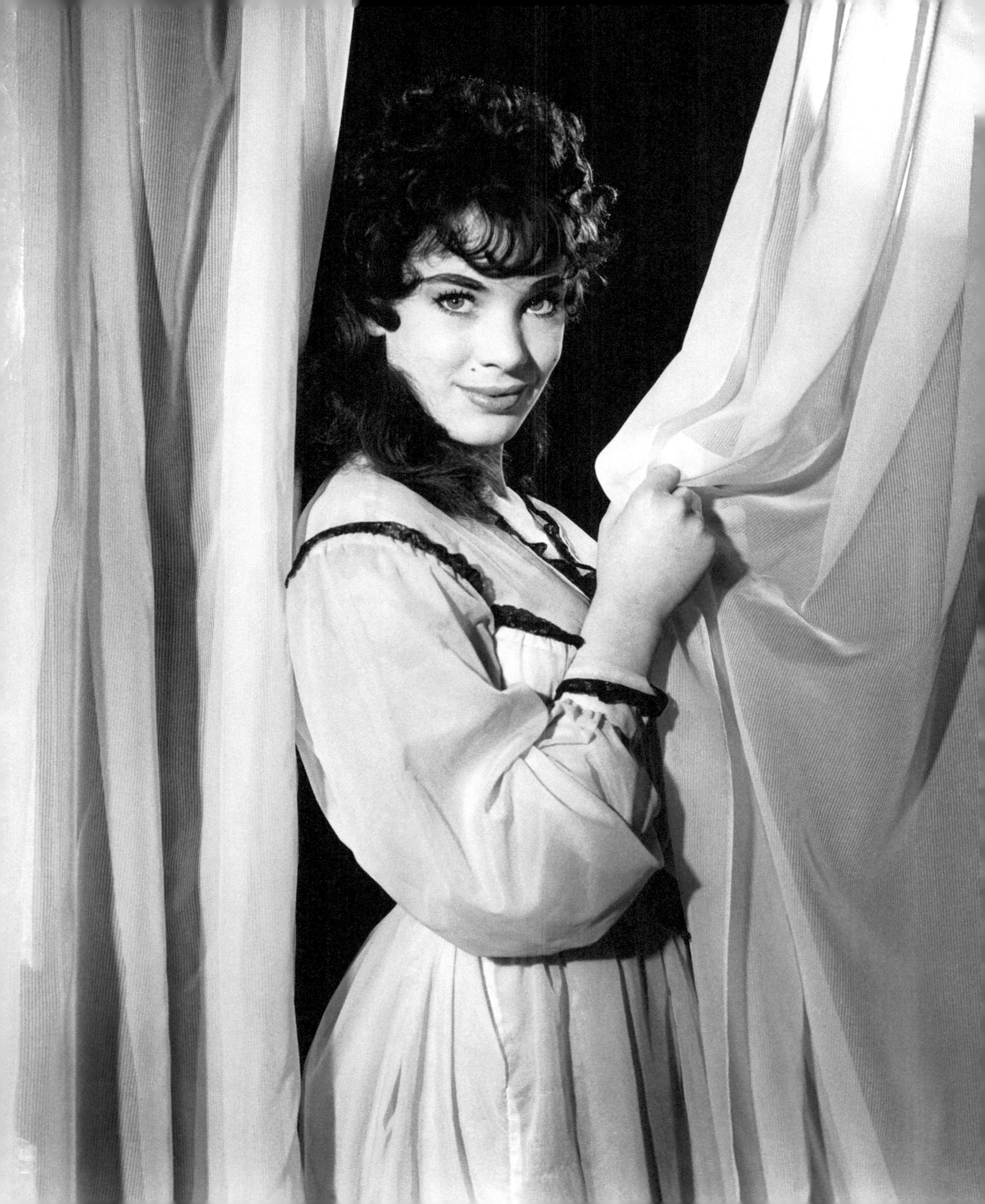

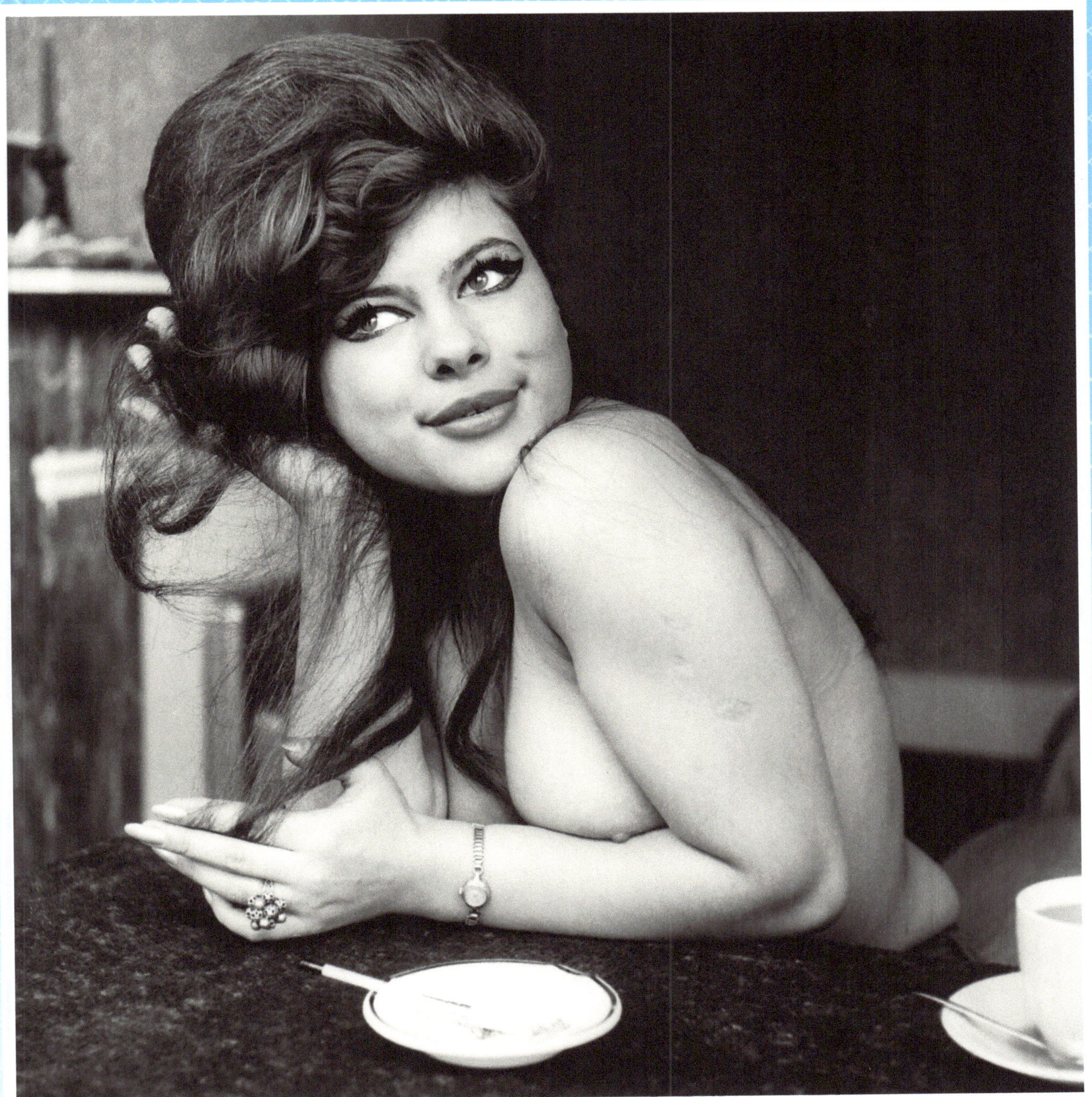

Above: Vera Novak was born in the former Yugoslavia – near Skopje (now the capital of Macedonia). Her father was critical of the Tito regime, and fled to Greece in 1950, never to be heard of officially again. This left Vera and her mother in a tough situation, and in desperation they moved to Rijeka, where Vera's mother felt she could earn enough to keep them alive by selling goods on the black market. As the wife and daughter of a known anti-Communist, the pair were under constant surveillance; their first attempt to escape to Italy resulted in their capture and 14 days in jail. Later, they were more fortunate. Having passed Trieste, they were horrified when stopped by police on what they thought was still Yugoslav soil; however, they had crossed the frontier and the police were Italian. Then came a spell in a camp at Salerno — "a part of my life I would like to forget," as Vera remarked. Finally, mother and daughter were allowed to leave the camp and travel to England, where they settled in Bournemouth. Vera's looks and figure soon brought in modelling and film work offers. She had a bit part in the feature film *The Beauty Jungle* (1964), and she also appeared in *The Naked World of Harrison Marks* (1966).

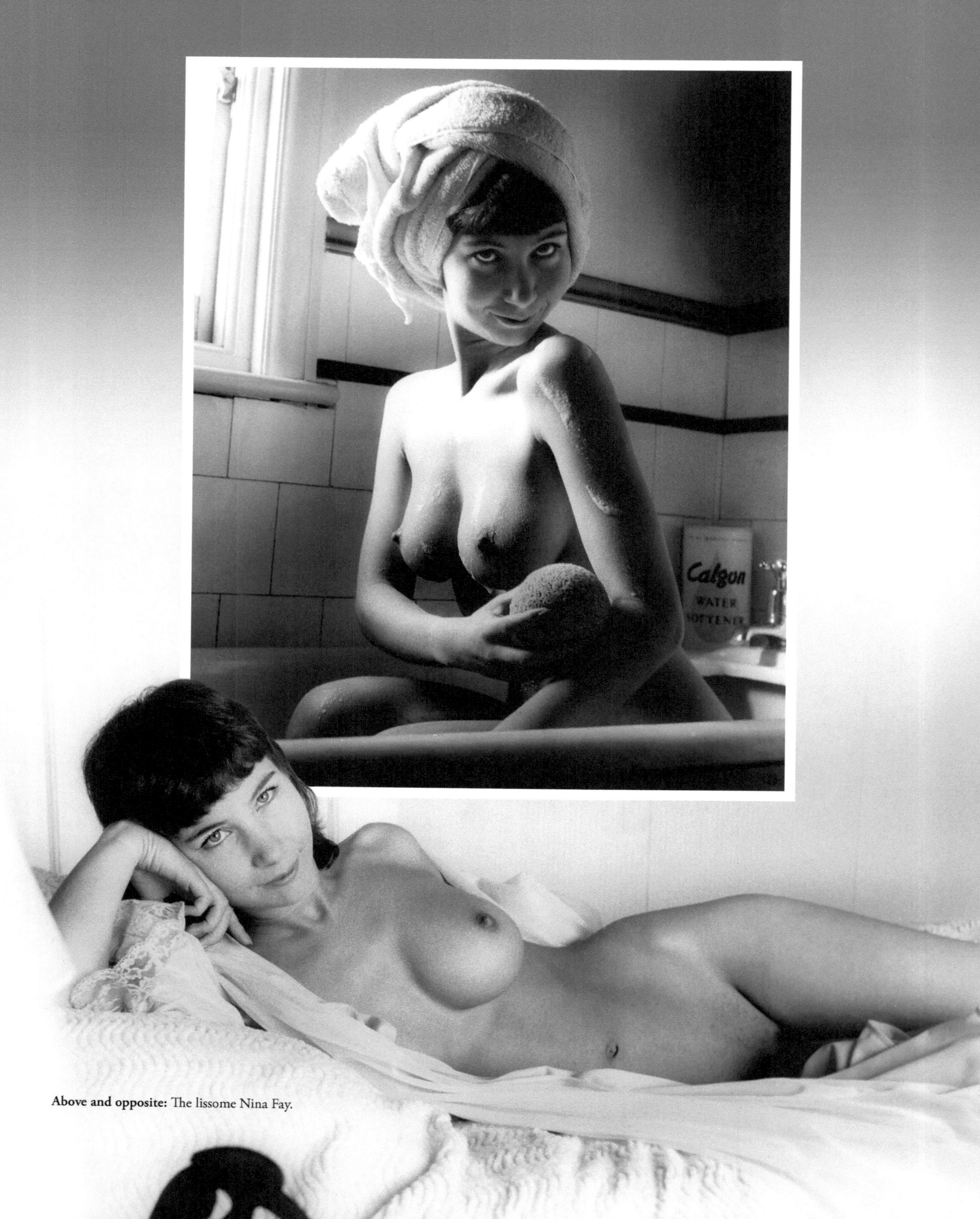

Above and opposite: The lissome Nina Fay.

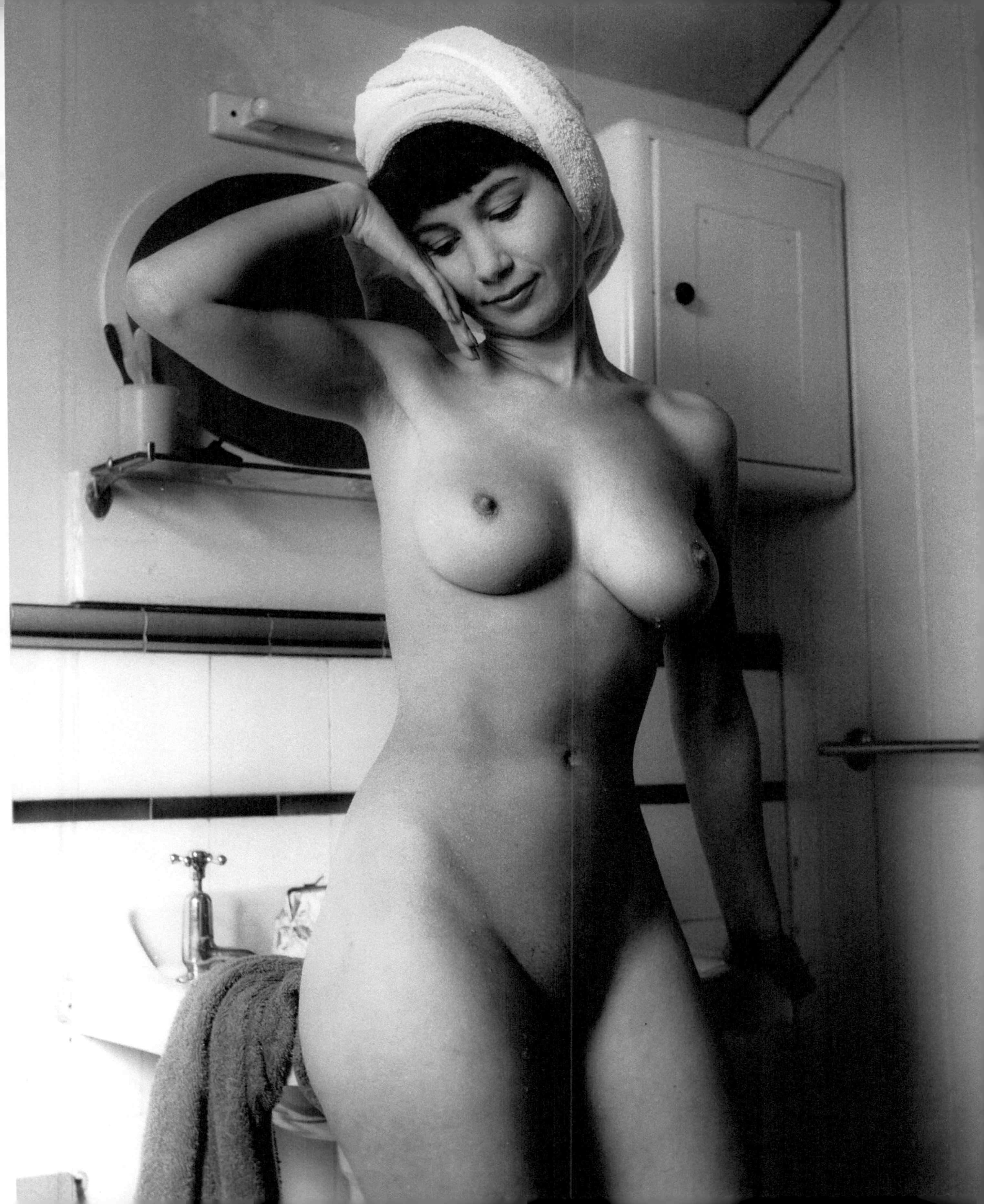

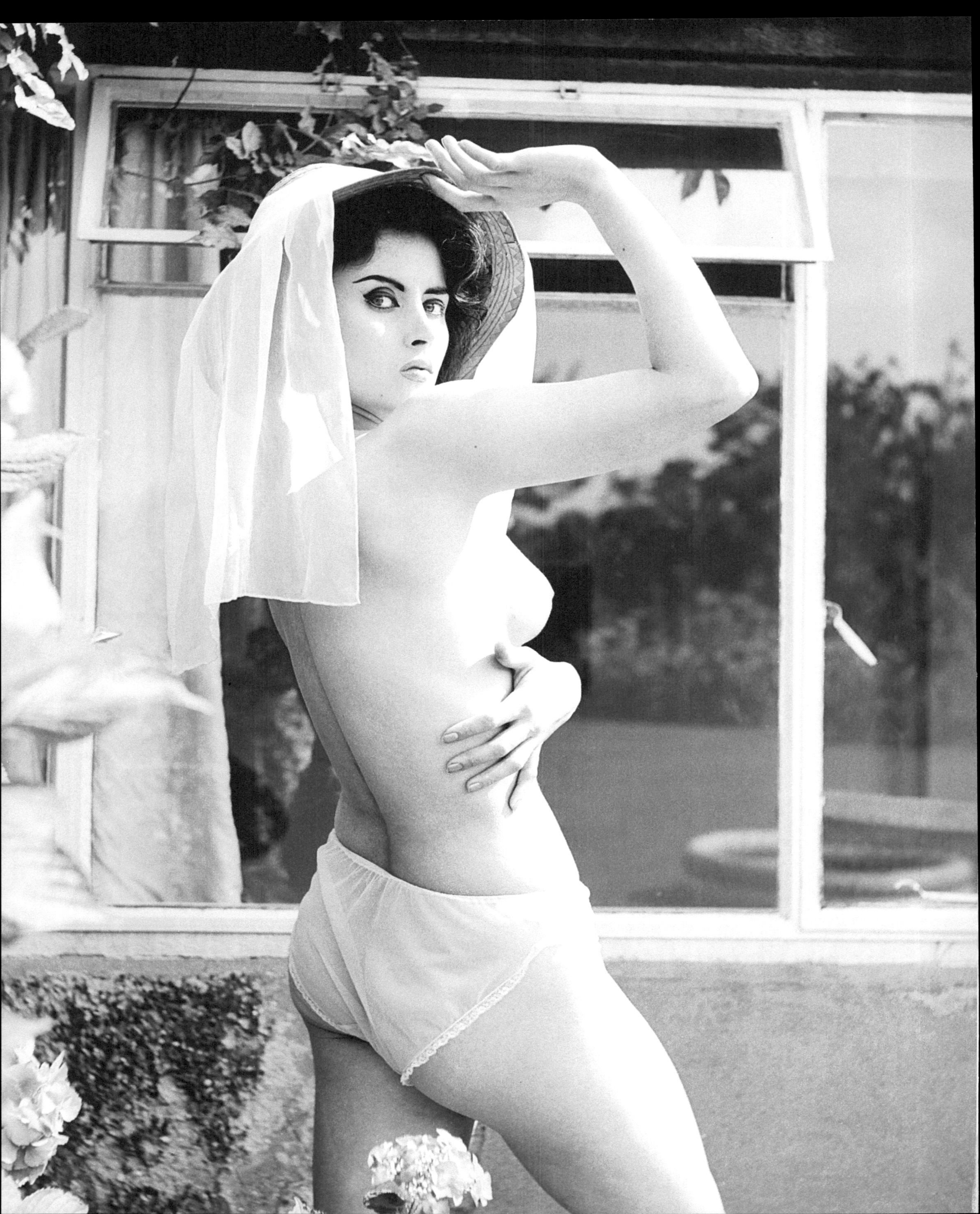

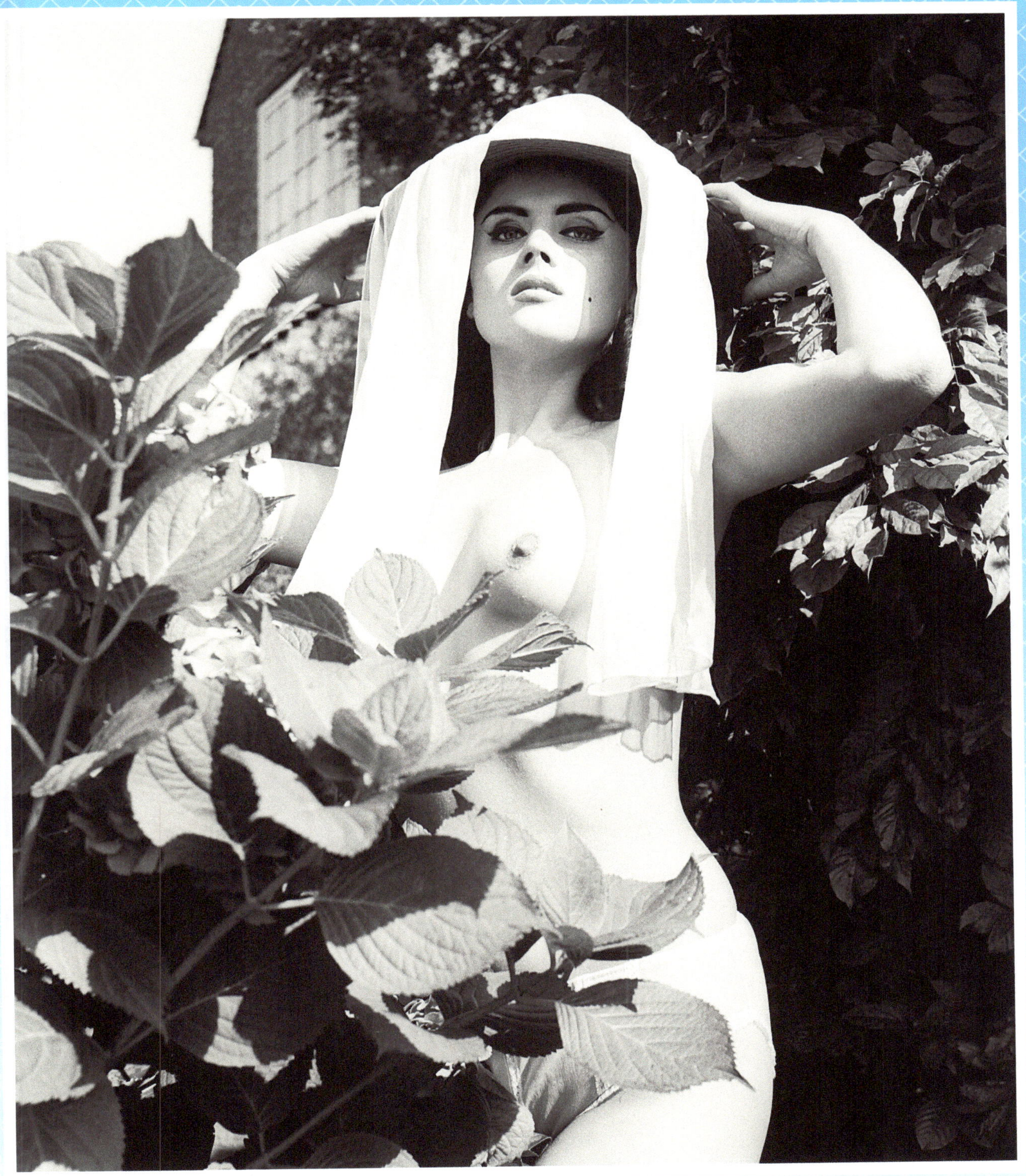

Above and opposite: The popular model Sophie Dawn, who appeared in the striptease films *The Bare Truth* (1964) and *Nature's Intention* (1964) by Kamera Cine Films and the book *She Walks in Beauty* (1964) by George Harrison Marks.

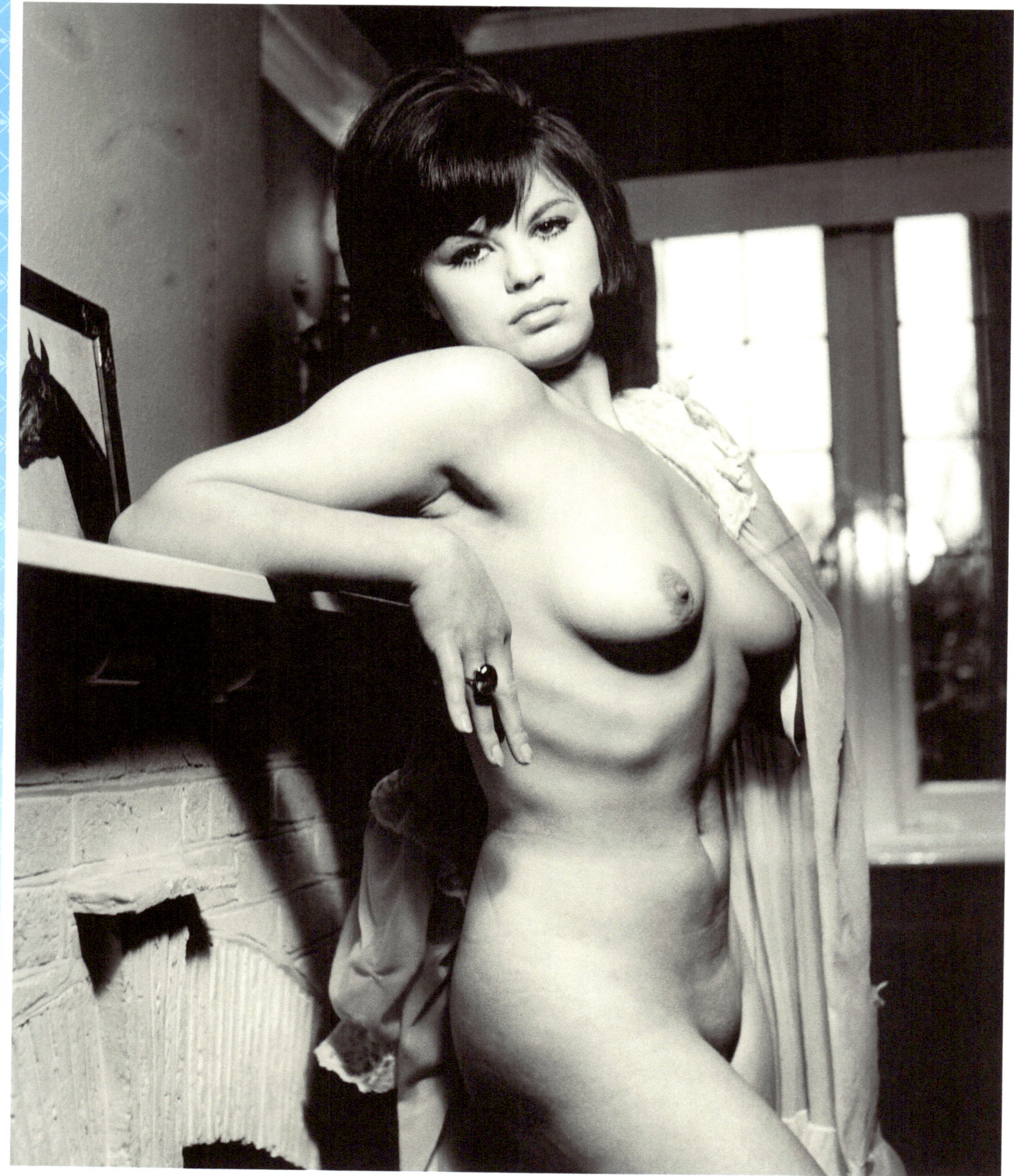

Above and opposite: Vivienne Warren, who married George Harrison Marks in 1963, after which she gave up her short-lived modelling career.

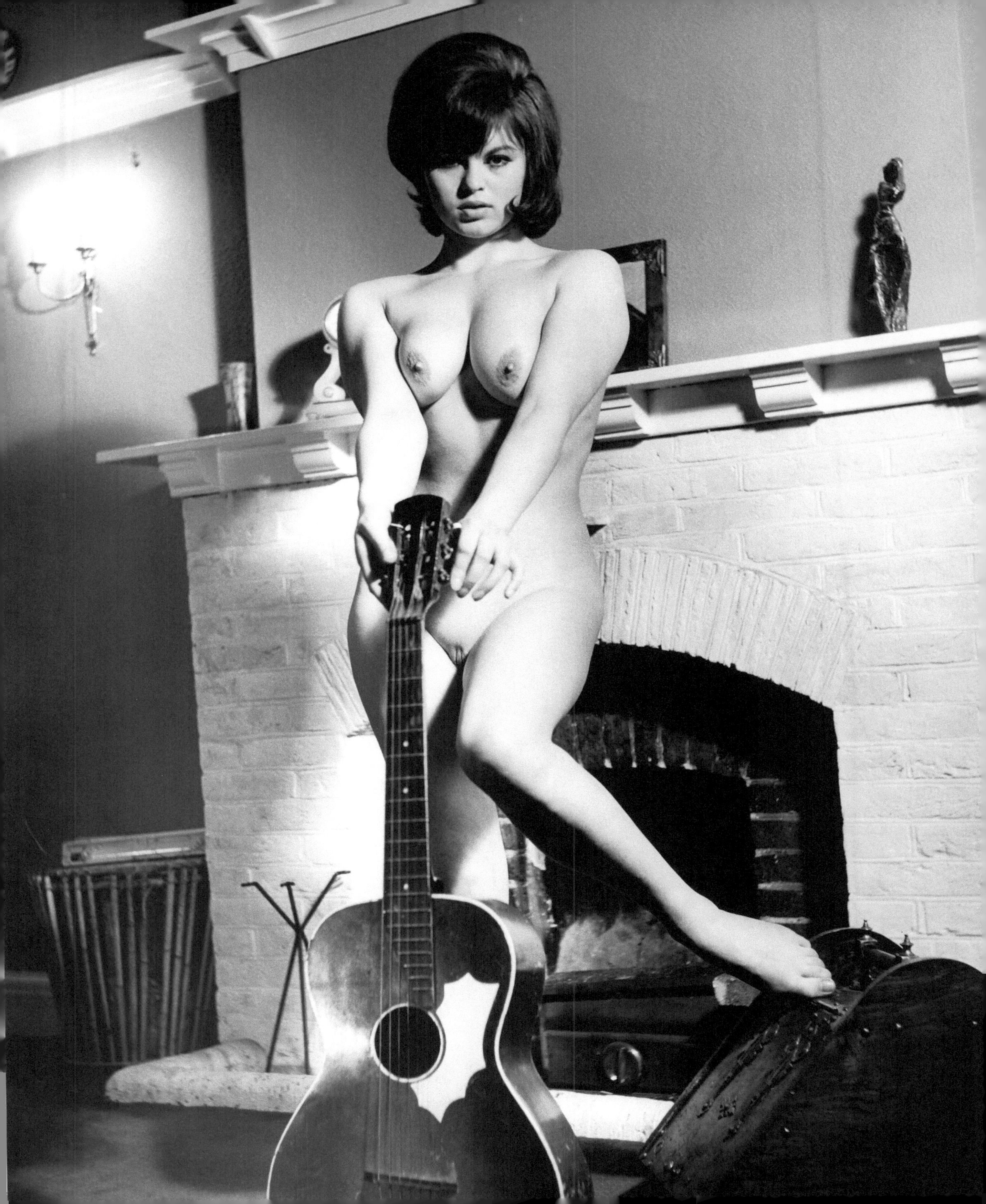

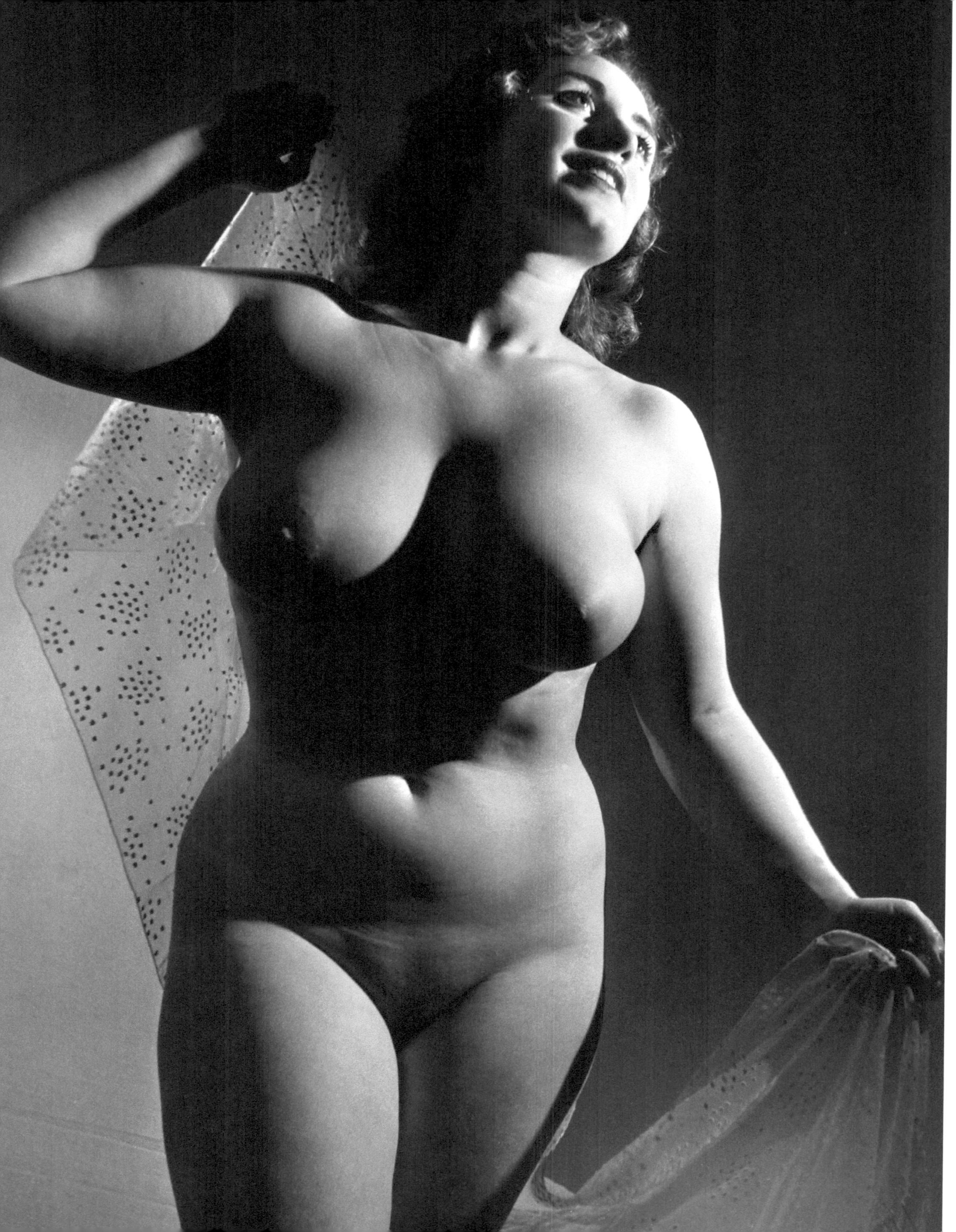

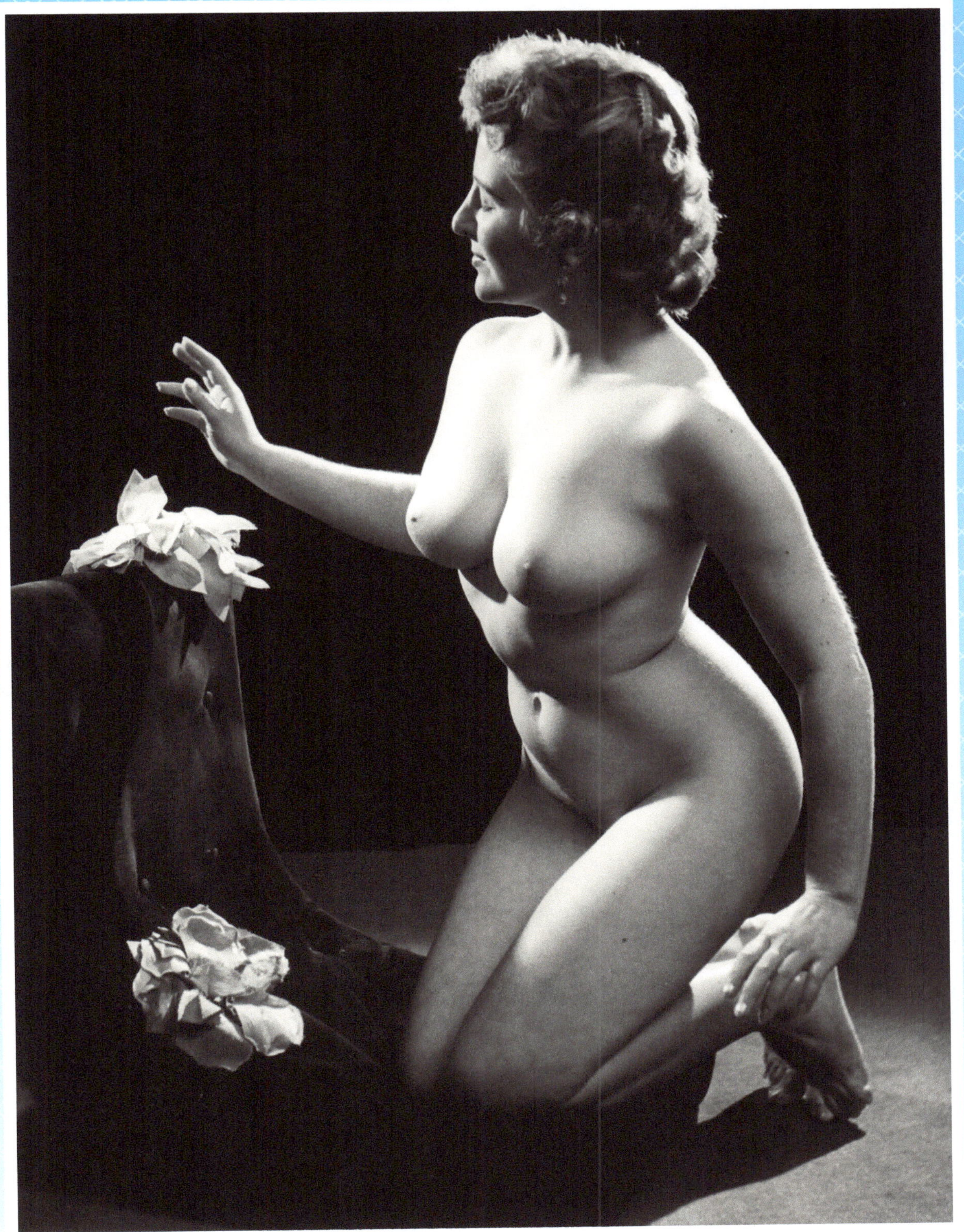

Above: Norma Forrest. **Opposite:** Valerie Williams.

WOLFBAIT
UNDER THE COUNTER CULTURE

ALSO AVAILABLE

Cinema au Naturel
A history of nudist film.

Miniten: Rules of the Game
Invented in the 1930s, Miniten is a
tennis-like game played by naturists.

Naked as Nature Intended
The epic tale of a nudist picture by
Pamela Green, with photographs by
Douglas "Dambuster" Webb, DFM.

The Naked Truth About Harrison Marks
The notorious biography by Franklyn Wood.

Past Masters of the Nude
An illustrated bibliography of nude photography
books published in England from 1896 to 1960.

Slide Show
A luscious look at the photographic slides
of Harrison Marks.

X-ray Specs and Other Vintage Ads
NEW!
A unique treasure chest of vintage advertising,
full of tease and prurient silliness.

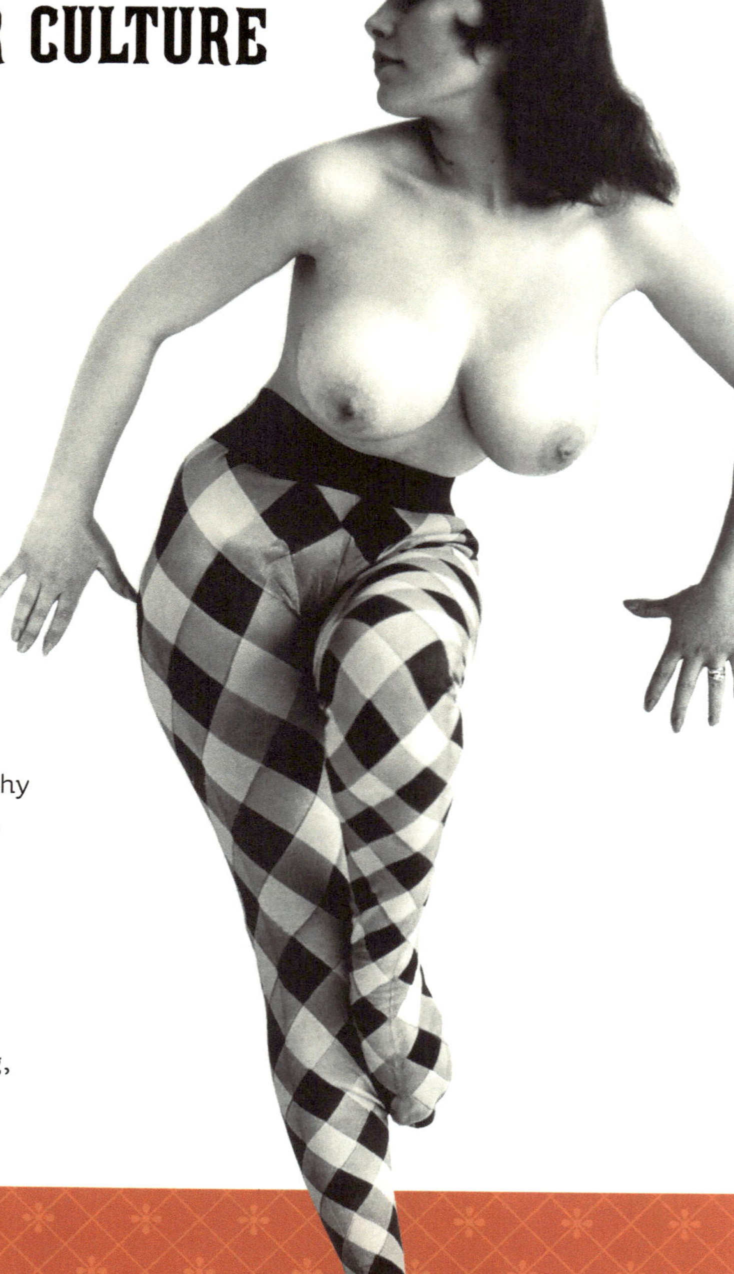

Doing Rude Things

The history of the British sex film.

NEW!
The Glamour Camera of Eva Grant

A short biography of Eva Grant, one of the world's foremost female figure photographers of the 1950s and 1960s, accompanied by a selection of some of her most captivating work.

NEW!
Glamour Model Revue

Featuring June Palmer, Paula Page and Tina Madison.

THE STEPHEN GLASS COLLECTION

Amazons of Yesteryear

A rare, action-packed collection of images of wrestling women of the 1940s and 1950s.

Beauty Off-Duty

Relaxed, everyday moments caught on camera.

Naked in the Menagerie

A playful look at Eve accompanied by her animal friends.

Nudist Camp Follies – volumes 1 and 2

An intimate look at the natural and free atmosphere in Sun Clubs.

Nymphs and Naiads

Beauty unadorned and outdoors.

Poise and Pose

A magnificent series of photographs of female beauty taken in the studio.

Order online at wolfbait.co.uk

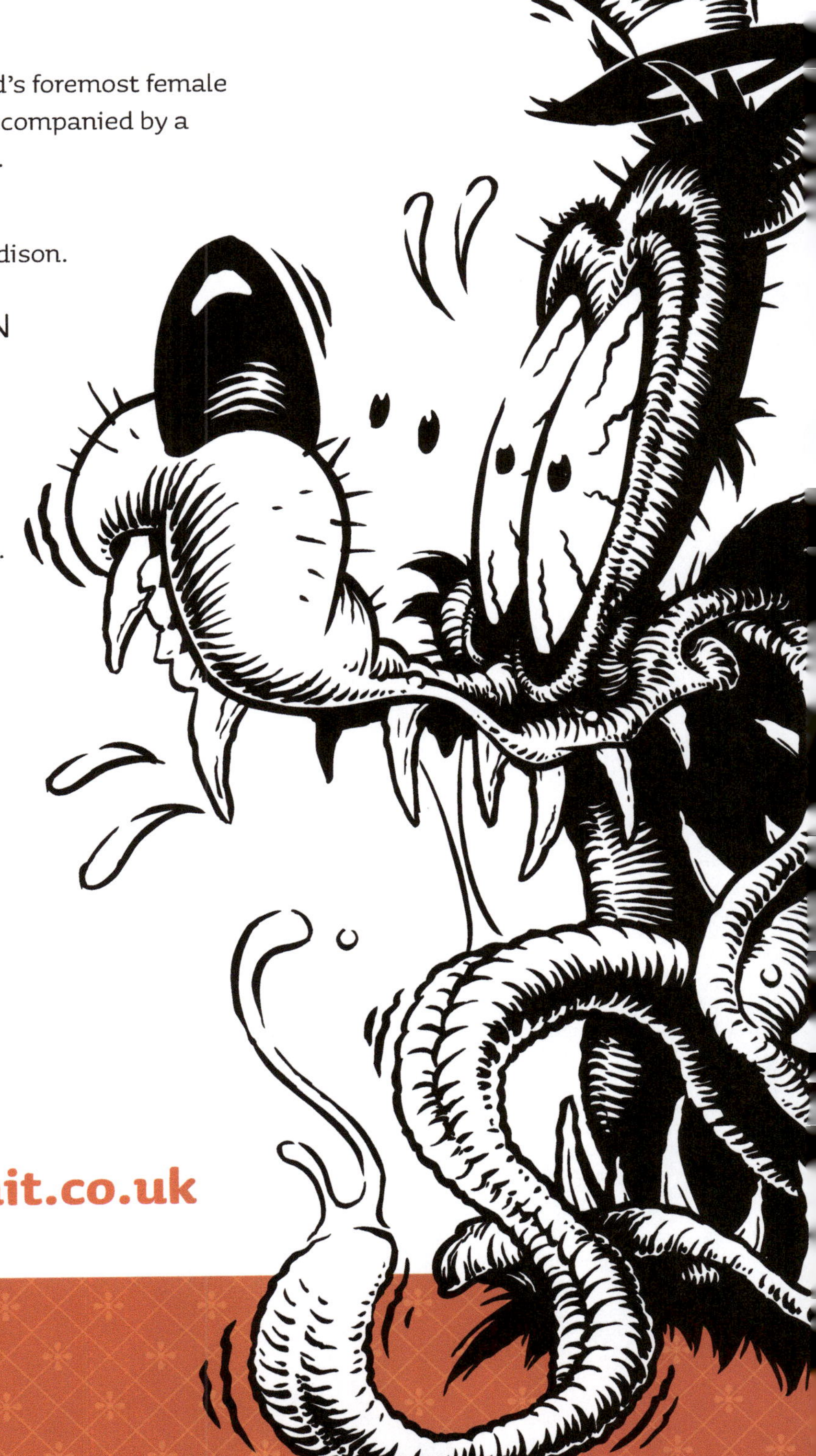

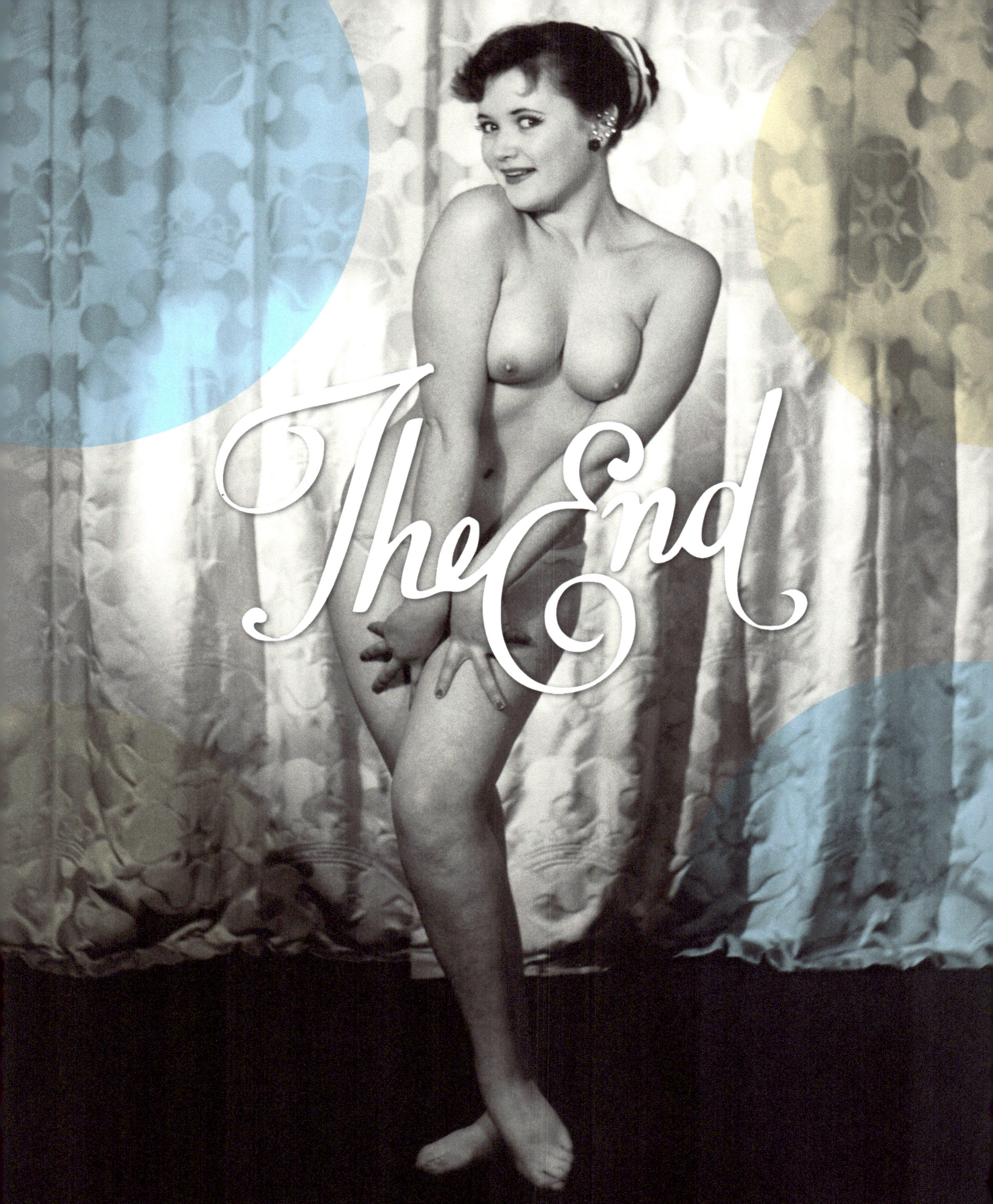
The End